Victorious

How To Face, Fight, and Finish Your Battles

Dr. John Polis

Victorious
How to Face, Fight, and Finish Your Battles
By John Polis
©2018 John Polis
Printed in the United States of America

ISBN 978-0-9898310-6-2

CONTENTS

Endorsements

It is so refreshing to read a book written through the filter of victorious living that God's Word teaches us we should have. This book shows us how to live out what it means to be the head only, and above only, and not beneath. This book gives us a strategy to identify our giants, overcome them, and walk in victory as a lifestyle not just a one-time event. Thank you, Dr. John, for the spirit of victory that is on your life.

Timothy Polis
Pastor - The Heights City Church, Arden NC
Certified John Maxwell Coach
youleadunlimited.com

We, in the Body of Christ, will greatly benefit by understanding who God has made us to be and the weapons that God has given us to use against the enemy. Dr. John Polis has revealed to us the purpose and plan of the battles we face, and this book will help us win so that no weapon formed against us will prosper.

Karen Ford
Administrator, Faith Church International
Master Financial Coach
karenford.org

This book is a must read by everyone! It is powerful, purposeful, and inspirational. The book was given to me at a time when I needed it the most. It has given me protection against the devil's attacks; rest assured those attacks are numerous. Reading and focusing on examples of how others such as David, Moses, and Paul experienced struggles throughout their lives, and they overcame because of their faith in the Lord, speaks volumes.

Reading this book is the most effective prescription for me when under attack. It reminds me of the armor that only God can provide through Jesus Christ and the Holy Spirit. Yes, the battles have already been won. NOW it is my turn to use what God has given me, by His grace, every minute of the day. The Word of God and examples as illustrated in this book give me peace and strength to continue, never give up, and live a victorious life.

So, when I am feeling sorry for myself, I think and speak of the examples throughout the Bible as illustrated in "Victorious" and realized I have been blessed by God. Thank you, Dr. John, for this amazing book.

Steve Haning
Certified Financial Consultant
Former President of Clarksburg Uptown,

an economic development group

We all will sooner or later face battles in our lives...but are we prepared to fight them and come out victorious? In his 40 years of global ministry, Dr. John Polis has effectively practiced what he is sharing in this latest book. Using the story of David and Goliath in 1 Samuel 17, he takes the reader step by step through a proven battle plan that addresses our identity in Christ, the supernatural power of the Holy Spirit and the working knowledge of God's Word, all to help the reader grow to their full faith potential. Every time we see a battle won, our faith grows a little stronger. This is the victory that overcomes the world even our faith [1 John 5:4]. The issue is not whether we're going to face a battle, the issue is are we prepared to face a battle. This book will give you that preparation.

Dr. Pat Polis
Certified Church Consultant
John Maxwell Team member

An inspiring book that offers insight and direction when found in spiritual warfare. A confidence builder to fight the good fight! To know "no weapon" (Is: 54:17) is truth.

I have served under Dr. Polis for 31 years and consider him as a military General in his teachings and leadership. It is an honor to recommend this book to you for your spiritual growth.

Ken Wright
CFO Faith Church International
Senior's Pastor

Apostle John Polis's new book, Victorious, is revelatory! It is a compilation of revelations on faith from scripture and the experiences of a man who lives and ministers in the faith realm.

Apostle Polis recognizes that as Christians we live in an adversarial world of warfare that comes in the form of temptations, sickness, problems, conflicts, and much more. Yet, our weaponry contains a great shield of protection - - the shield of faith!

Victorious will equip you to live, move, and have your being within the realm of faith. You will definitely go from faith to faith; from the good faith that you are in now, to a greater faith as you progressively read each chapter.

This book is a must-read for all believers who desire to be men and women of great faith with God as their firm foundation.

Dr. John P. Kelly
Convener, International Coalition of Apostolic Leaders

Foreward

STAND FIRM

When I first heard Dr. Polis' messages on Isaiah 54:17, I paused and took the time to inventory my life and journey of faith. I thought about how often I had ignored God's voice, backed down, or simply given up on a leading from Christ because I allowed the enemy's attacks to distract or dissuade me. What an encouragement and equipping tool Polis' message is for me and will be for you!

When caught up in the passion of preaching and teaching God's truths, I really believe without reservations what I am saying. But in the dark moments of spiritual warfare, my personal doubts and fears often sabotage my ability to fully trust God's ways or my willingness to do what God desires. It's one thing to declare and shout the victory; it's another thing for us to battle from the trenches of life's struggles and disappointments.

I found Polis' "Victorious" to be soul food and Spirit fire for me. His teaching and equipping in the following pages helped me and will empower you to understand the devices of the enemy and how to stand firm in Christ to overcome every obstacle or temptation spiritual and human detractors use to block your path to victorious living—being more than a conqueror through Christ Jesus.

In this book, I discovered how to face the attack and fight the good fight of faith being filled with the Spirit. I was encouraged to finish the battle and do what God required of me in each battle. Certainly, the battle belongs to the Lord; but I must focus and face it, fight through it, and finish as I am exercising my faith and putting on God's armor.

I highly recommend you pause your busy schedule, take a mini, spiritual retreat, turning off all your device and study this book with your journal in hand, and allow yourself to be filled with the wisdom, knowledge, and understanding that Dr. John Polis shares in "Victorious."

Dr. Larry Keefauver
Salem Publishing
YMCS - Author Coaching, Publishing Services

Introduction

FACE IT - FIGHT IT - FINISH IT

"No weapon formed against you shall prosper, and every tongue which rises against you in judgment You shall condemn. This is the heritage of the servants of the Lord, and their righteousness is from Me," says the Lord. (Isaiah 54:17)

The children of Israel were being released from Babylonian captivity and returning to their homeland. God gave them a promise that as long as they would walk with Him, no weapon formed against them will prosper and their future be full of victory. The word "prosper" here means *to succeed or fulfill its intended purpose.*

The Expanded Bible translation of Isaiah 54:17 says, *"'So no weapon that is used [forged] against you will defeat*

7

you [succeed]. You will show that those who speak against you are wrong [refute every accusation against you; refute every tongue that rises against you in judgment]. These are the good things [heritage] my servants receive. Their victory [vindication; righteousness] comes from me,' says the Lord."

We have that same promise because we were freed from captivity when we were born again. Whatever our battles, whether they are physical, emotional, or spiritual, no weapon of any kind can defeat us as long as we are walking with God. Notice, though, God was telling the Israelites and He is telling us we are going to come up against judgmental people and potentially destructive situations. In fact, Jesus warned us in John 16:33, *"These things I've spoken to you that in me you may have peace. In the world you shall have tribulation; but be of good cheer I have overcome the world."*

We need to be aware that there is an enemy roaming about as a roaring lion (1 Peter 5:8) whose whole purpose is to steal our peace, destroy our heritage, and kill us (John 10:10).

WHEN SATAN COMES AGAINST US... **AND HE WILL...**

WHEN THE DEVIL DEVISES WEAPONS TO ATTACK US... **AND HE DOES ALL THE TIME...**

WHEN HE COMES AGAINST US TO TEMPT AND DESTROY US...EVEN KILL US... **AND THAT'S HIS NON-ENDING MISSION...**

THE WEAPONS OF THE ENEMY OF OUR SOUL **CANNOT COME TO FRUITION.**

The moment we were born again, children of the **Most High God**, Christ set us free from captivity, out of the Egypt of our bondage to sin, along with its power to destroy our peace, plans, and purpose.

THE DEVIL IS DEFEATED! NO WEAPON FORMED AGAINST US BY HIM, OUR ENEMIES, OR THE WORLD CAN SUCCEED...UNLESS WE LET IT!

There are people and situations in the world that will come against us and accuse us seeking to defeat us. We will face battles in our lives, but God has given us everything we need to confidently face these battles, effectively fight against any enemy, and finish victoriously.

Finally, my brothers be strong in the Lord and in the power of His might. Put on the whole armor of God, that you may be able to stand against the wiles of the devil. For we do not wrestle against flesh and blood but against principalities, against the powers, against the rulers of the darkness of this age, against spiritual host of wickedness in the heavenly places. (Ephesians 6:10-12)

God is assuring us just as He did Joshua as he prepared to lead the Israelites into their Promised Land, *"Be strong and of good courage; do not be afraid, nor be dismayed, for the Lord your God is with you wherever you go"* (Joshua 1:9).

At this moment, you may be under spiritual attack. Your emotions of fear, doubt, worry, and uncertainty may be raging out of control. This book is your guide for hearing God's truth about yourself and the enemy. You will discover how to...

- Face head on the enemy and the weapons with which he is bombarding you.
- Fight the good fight of faith without faltering or retreating.
- Be Filled with Holy Spirit power and confidence to persevere through every trial, overcome every setback.
- And finish strong and victoriously.

Chapter 1

FACE IT: DAVID AND GOLIATH

But understand this, that in the last days dangerous times [of great stress and trouble] will come [difficult days that will be hard to bear]. (2 Timothy 3:1 AMP)

Difficult, fierce, dangerous, and hard to endure times are coming; we cannot avoid, ignore, or escape them. Even though God has promised us no weapon formed against will succeed, we've got to do our part. Just like all the promises God has given us, we are to be active participants. In this case, we are called to confront those problems head on. They are not just going to disappear without a fight! God expects us to use what He has given us and trust that He will guide us into victory.

The most epic battle in scripture where someone faced

inhuman possibilities was David's battle with the giant Goliath. There are three things we can learn from this biblical example.

WE NEED TO FACE THE BATTLE.

WE NEED TO FIGHT THE BATTLE.

WE NEED TO FINISH THE BATTLE.

FACE IT, FIGHT IT, AND FINISH IT.

FACE IT

Then David said to Saul, "Let no man's heart fail because of him; your servant will go and fight with this Philistine." (1 Samuel 17:32)

So, first and foremost, we have to **face...confront... enter...and fight** the battle. You know why? You can't escape it. David, said, "Somebody's got to face this situation. It isn't going to go away." Tammy Baker wrote a book called, "You've Got to Run to The Roar." Lions roar. When the other animals hear that roar, it paralyzes them and makes them easy prey.

That's what Satan does, too. 1 Peter 5:8 warns us, *"Be sober, be vigilant; because your adversary the devil walks about **like a roaring lion**, seeking whom he may devour"*

(NKJV emphasis added). Fear will come against us so powerfully that we'll be paralyzed and won't know what to do. His goal is to freak us out, stir up fear with us, cause us to panic and run from the battle instead of facing it.

What frightens you? What makes you latch onto the instinct for flight instead of fight? You run instead of engaging in the fight because of...

- ✓ Past defeats and failures? **Saint, you cannot fail unless you run and quit.**
- ✓ Broken relationships? **Child of God, your relationships can heal through forgiveness, restoration, and reconciliation.**
- ✓ Lack of confidence? **Woman or Man of God, grow up...stop acting like babe in Christ and be who you are empowered to be...a soldier, a warrior in Christ's army.**
- ✓ Poor self-identity? **Christian, you are being transformed into the identity of Christ, you belong to Christ, get over yourself...die to your old self, walk as a new creation in Christ.**

The Bible declares that in these last days, we will face difficult, fierce, and hard situations. We're living in tribulation now. Jesus reminds us that in this world we will have tribulation, but be of good cheer, we have overcome the world!

We see the roaring lion using the anti-Christ spirit to bring in lawlessness. Brutal, unspeakable things are being done by the Islamic State in Iraq and Syria (ISIS) with the purpose of causing terror in the hearts of God's people. We can't just turn off the reports and hide from them. When we see children and young adults going onto school campuses and killing fellow students, we need to realize we have a problem that needs to be faced and dealt with in a definitive way.

> *Then as he talked with them, there was the champion, the Philistine of Gath, Goliath by name, coming up from the armies of the Philistines; and he spoke according to the same words. So David heard them. And all the men of Israel, when they saw the man, fled from him and were dreadfully afraid. (1 Samuel 17:23-24)*

What we are witnessing here is a classic enemy tactic. Send out the most intimidating "champion" they have and scare the opposition so bad they just turn tail and run away. David could not believe what he was seeing. *"Your Majesty,"* he said, *"this Philistine shouldn't turn us into cowards. I'll go out and fight him myself!"* (1 Samuel 17:32 CEV). David's brothers saw him only as an arrogant shepherd boy who should go back and tend the sheep.

> *Now Eliab his oldest brother heard when he spoke to the men and Eliab's anger was aroused against David and he said, "Why did you come down here? And with whom have you left those few sheep in the wilderness? I know your pride and insults of your heart for you have come down to see the battle." And*

David said, "What have I done now? Is there
not a cause?" (1 Samuel 17:28-29)

David's brothers and all the armies of Israel were paralyzed with fear when they heard Goliath roar. When David asked them why they weren't facing the battle, they accused him of having pride and arrogance in his heart instead of recognizing his true motive. He had true devotion for God and couldn't let this "devil" keep roaring and blaspheming God without doing something about it.

And Saul said to David, You are not able to go
up against this Philistine to fight with him: for
you are but a youth. (1 Samuel 17:33)

What his brothers and the king did not understand was David had learned to trust God as he was all alone out in the fields defending his father's sheep against a lion and a bear. In seemingly impossible situations, David had learned to use the weapons God had provided and had confidence God had his back.

But David said to Saul, "Your servant used to
keep his father's sheep, and when a lion or a
bear came and took a lamb out of the flock, I
went out after it and struck it, and delivered
the lamb from its mouth; and when it arose
against me, I caught it by its beard, and struck
and killed it. Your servant has killed both lion
and bear; and this uncircumcised Philistine
will be like one of them, seeing he has defied

the armies of the living God." Moreover David said, "The Lord, who delivered me from the paw of the lion and from the paw of the bear, He will deliver me from the hand of this Philistine." And Saul said to David, "Go, and the Lord be with you!" (1 Samuel 17:34-37)

WE NEED TO FACE OUR BATTLE BECAUSE IT'S NOT GOING AWAY. WE NEED TO OVERCOME OUR FEAR OF THE ENEMY AND REALIZE HE CAN ONLY ROAR.

Reinhard Bonnke said, "The Bible says that the devil is like a roaring lion (1 Peter 5:8). He comes in the darkness and tries to frighten the children of God with his mighty roar. But when you switch on the light of the Word of God, you discover that there is no lion. There is only a mouse with a microphone! The devil is an imposter. Got it?"

Like the fearful soldiers David questioned, we often don't want to face life as it is. We hide, blame, and ignore the situation, but the fact of the matter is, the problem is not going away. Goliath wasn't going away just because they weren't willing to face him. Our problems won't go away just because we're unwilling to face them.

WHAT KEEPS US FROM FACING OUR PROBLEMS?

There are several things that become apparent in this

biblical account of David and Goliath. The first reason that we see is fear. Satan "roared" at the Israelites using Goliath, a man of great size and strength to strike fear in the hearts of the soldiers of Saul's army. 1 Samuel 17:4-11 describes what Goliath looked like and what his intimidating presence did to Saul and all the Israelites.

> Then Goliath, a Philistine champion from Gath, came out of the Philistine ranks to face the forces of Israel. He was over nine feet tall! He wore a bronze helmet, and his bronze coat of mail weighed 125 pounds. He also wore bronze leg armor, and he carried a bronze javelin on his shoulder. The shaft of his spear was as heavy and thick as a weaver's beam, tipped with an iron spearhead that weighed 15 pounds. His armor bearer walked ahead of him carrying a shield. Goliath stood and shouted a taunt across to the Israelites. "Why are you all coming out to fight?" he called. "I am the Philistine champion, but you are only the servants of Saul. Choose one man to come down here and fight me! If he kills me, then we will be your slaves. But if I kill him, you will be our slaves! I defy the armies of Israel today! Send me a man who will fight me!" When Saul and the Israelites heard this, they were terrified and deeply shaken. (NLT)

Are you constantly challenged by a rotten person

or circumstance in life? Goliath came every morning and every evening for forty days before David arrived on the scene. Every day the same thing happened. The soldiers from King Saul's army lined up for battle, Goliath came out and challenged them, and they all ran and hid from him.

Do you feel insecure, incapable, or overwhelmed? Another issue that could keep us from facing our problems is lack of confidence in ourselves or in God. David did not have this problem. In fact, his brothers thought he was over confident in himself. However, he knew God had been training him and grooming him to be prepared for facing Goliath. He also had learned he could put his confidence in God. When he faced the roaring giant, he boldly declared his confidence in the God he served.

> Then David said to the Philistine, "You come to me with a sword, with a spear, and with a javelin. But I come to you in the name of the Lord of hosts, the God of the armies of Israel, whom you have defied. This day the Lord will deliver you into my hand, and I will strike you and take your head from you. And this day I will give the carcasses of the camp of the Philistines to the birds of the air and the wild beasts of the earth, that all the earth may know that there is a God in Israel. Then all this assembly shall know that the Lord does not save with sword and spear; for the battle is the Lord's, and He will give you into our hands." So it was, when the Philistine arose

and came and drew near to meet David, that David hurried and ran toward the army to meet the Philistine. (1 Samuel 17:45-48)

David not only declared his confidence in God, he put action to his declaration. As roaring Goliath came at him, he ran toward the Philistine. He confidently faced his enemy knowing no weapon formed against him could prosper when he was serving Almighty God.

Are you too proud to seek help from Christ and Christian brothers and sisters? A third issue that could be keeping us from facing our problem is pride. We don't want to look bad in front of others. Once again, we can look at how David chose to face Goliath. When King Saul finally agreed to allow David to go against Goliath, he tried to outfit David to look like the king's champion.

So Saul clothed David with his armor, and he put a bronze helmet on his head; he also clothed him with a coat of mail. David fastened his sword to his armor and tried to walk, for he had not tested them. And David said to Saul, "I cannot walk with these, for I have not tested them." So David took them off. Then he took his staff in his hand; and he chose for himself five smooth stones from the brook, and put them in a shepherd's bag, in a pouch which he had, and his sling was in his hand. And he drew near to the Philistine. (1 Samuel 17:38-40 KJV)

David needed to do things the way God had told him to. It didn't matter if his brothers, the other soldiers, or the other army thought he looked foolish. As a matter of fact, that was the last tactic his enemy used against him. As Goliath approached David all dressed up in his fine battle gear, he began to mock the young shepherd boy and make fun of the way he looked.

> *So the Philistine came, and began drawing near to David, and the man who bore the shield went before him. And when the Philistine looked about and saw David, he disdained him; for he was only a youth, ruddy and good-looking. So the Philistine said to David, "Am I a dog, that you come to me with sticks?" And the Philistine cursed David by his gods. And the Philistine said to David, "Come to me, and I will give your flesh to the birds of the air and the beasts of the field!" (1 Samuel 17:41-44)*

We may be struggling with financial problems that are just astronomical, but we won't tell anybody or reach out for any help because we're afraid of what they might think of us. Pride not only stops us from facing many problems, it can keep us from reaching out for the help that we need. We come to church looking good, smiling, and looking like everything is fine because we are afraid somebody might look down on us or think evil of us if they know we have a problem.

Unfortunately, the financial problems don't go away

because you ignore them; those marital problems don't go away because you deny them; your child's addiction to drugs and alcohol won't get resolved by hiding the problem.

Satan would like nothing better than for you to run away, hide, deny, and ignore your problems. Yes, Satan is the god of this age, and he is prowling around like a hungry lion. He is even roaring loudly, but the truth is you don't need to fear him or any other enemy. God has promised you that no weapon formed against you will prosper when you are doing what He has called you to do.

> *Finally, my brothers be strong in the Lord and in the power of His might. Put on the whole armor of God, that you may be able to stand against the wiles of the devil. For we do not wrestle against flesh and blood but against principalities, against the powers, against the rulers of the darkness of this age (world), against spiritual host of wickedness in the heavenly places. (Ephesians 6:10-12)*

The Lord says you can't escape the problems of life because you are in a world that's got a system designed by an enemy who comes to steal, kill, and destroy. However, it's time for you and all the people of God to get up out of the trenches and stop hiding in fear. It is time for you to take on the mantle, the anointing, and the robe of David. As you use the weapons God has given you and employ the training He has put you through, you can confidently face and slay the Goliath's in your life.

So, my first encouragement for you is:

FACE YOUR PROBLEMS BECAUSE THEY WILL NOT MAGICALLY DISAPPEAR.

Remember that your reality isn't the Magic Kingdom; you are a soldier and citizen of the Kingdom of God!

SWALLOW YOUR PRIDE, BE DELIVERED FROM FEAR, AND GET BEYOND YOUR LACK OF SELF-CONFIDENCE.

FACE THE ATTACK HEAD-ON, BECAUSE GOD IS ON YOUR SIDE.

FACE IT, NEVER FEAR IT

For God has not given us a spirit of fear, but of power and of love and of a sound mind. (2 Timothy 1:7)

The opposite of "facing it" is "fearing it." Let's unpack a body-soul-spirit "how-to" process for overcoming fear and implementing "face it." Understand that fear never comes from God. Fear is a response from our soul (feelings, thoughts, and will) that has been learned from past experiences with people and situations. Others may have taught us fear. Past experiences that have resulted in being hurt, rejected, abandoned, abused, or injured in some way may have triggered a fearful response in our souls. We may have bought the enemy's lie that we should fear something or someone because we were weak or worthless. As a child of God, we are being transformed into a new creation—the image/identity of Christ and are being indwelt and continually filled with the Holy Spirit. That means we have within us the supernatural, miracle-working power (dunamis) to overcome all fear; the love (agape) that casts out all fear; and a sound, renewed mind (nous) to know not only the schemes of the world and the enemy but also the good plans of God to live as victors not victims.

Now, a body (action) - soul (feeling, thought, decision) - spirit (Spirited empowered gift and fruit - process for facing it not fearing is...

1. **Face It with "Us" not "Me, Myself, and I"** – The enemy seeks to destroy sheep by isolating them. His **lie** to you is that you must face that situation or person(s) all alone. The **truth** is that Christ never leaves or forsakes us. Our Good Shepherd is with us always even through the valley of the shadow of death. Note that the 2 Timothy 1:7 teaches, *"For God has not given us...."* That's plural not singular. Being not alone means that we are continually in covenant relationships with God-Other Believers-Me. God has surrounded us with a multitude of godly counselors to give us wisdom, knowledge, and understanding. We have saints to pray for us, encourage us, counsel us, resource us, and fight with us. We are not individual warriors going into

a fight but rather God's army fortified with angelic hosts.

ASK YOURSELF... "Who is the Lord providing for me, as my team, to prepare for a good fight?"

2. **Face It with Truth not Lies** – We are to speak the truth to ourselves and others in love; we invited others to speak the truth to us from God's word in love as well. Not being conformed to this world but being transformed by the renewing of our minds, we confront every enemy and problem with truth— the sword of the spirit. We are boldly confident in the Lord not walking according to the flesh, for the weapons of our warfare...are mighty in God for pulling down strongholds and casting down every argument within us and from others that does not align with God's truth about the issues facing us (2 Corinthians 10:1-6).

ASK YOURSELF... "What lies do I need to reject; what truths do I need for renewing my mind?"

3. **Face It with Confidence not Doubt, Uncertainty, and Worry.** We are not anxious about anything, but in everything by prayer with thanksgiving, we make our (not alone with but with others) requests known to God, and the peace that passes all understanding will guard our minds and hearts

through Christ Jesus (Philippians 4:6). When facing it, our confidence in the Lord not in ourselves and we will refuse to cast aside our confidence (Proverbs 3:26, Hebrews 10:35, 1 John 5:14).

ASK YOURSELF... *"What right decisions do I need to make now and what right people do I need with me now to ready myself for battle?"*

Facing it involves all three of the above steps so that we are prepared for battle. The tribulations, trials, sufferings, and tests in life don't go away...rather we face them and go through them victorious. Stop praying for the fight to disappear but rather for Christ with other saints to prepare you for the fight by willingly facing it. Facing it cleanses you as a vessel of honor, *"sanctified and useful for the Master, prepared for every good work"* (2 Timothy 2:21).

WHAT IS KEEPING YOU FROM FACING YOUR PROBLEM?

Before you move on to the next chapter, take the time to review what you have learned in this chapter. Answer the question and then begin to implement these powerful truths so you can become the David you have been called to be in God's army.

- Why do you have to face the problem?
- What fear has you so paralyzed you don't know what to do?

- What do you need to do to get beyond your lack of confidence in yourself?
- Why can you have complete confidence in God?
- Has pride kept you from dealing with your problem head on?

Swallow your pride, get delivered from fear, and get beyond that lack of self-confidence.

FACE IT! ... BECAUSE GOD IS ON YOUR SIDE AND NO WEAPON FORMED AGAINST YOU WILL PROSPER.

Chapter 2

FIGHT IT: MOSES

[1]*"Some Christians want enough of Christ to be identified with him but not enough to be seriously inconvenienced; they genuinely cling to basic Christian orthodoxy but do not want to engage in serious Bible study; they value moral probity, especially of the public sort, but do not engage in war against inner corruptions; they fret over the quality of the preacher's sermon but do not worry much over the quality of their own prayer life. Such Christians are content with mediocrity." – D. A. Carson*

1   D. A. Carson (1992). "A Call to Spiritual Reformation: Priorities from Paul and His Prayers", p.121, Baker Academic

DON'T SETTLE FOR LESS.

REFUSE TO BE SATISFIED WITH MEDIOCRITY OR WITH A PARTIAL VICTORY.

DON'T BE CONTENT UNTIL YOU HAVE COMPLETELY TRIUMPHED!

Whatever battle you're going through in your life, resolve to fully solve the problem, vanquish the enemy, and completely dismiss the issue. Determine that every negative feeling associated with the battle is erased from your soul. Cultivate the fruit of the Spirit as the continual harvest in your relationships going forward. Declare this:

> *This is the victory that overcomes the world - our faith! (1 John 5:4)*

David didn't know when he fought that lion that he was going to have to fight a bear next. When he fought that lion, something happened on the inside of him that prepared him for the bear. After fighting the lion and the bear, he was ready when his giant appeared—Goliath.

You can't kill a giant with just "lion faith" or "bear faith." The way you get "giant faith" is by fighting battles and growing stronger and stronger throughout your life.

> *"Count it all joy when you go through various trials knowing that the trying of your faith*

worketh endurance so that you may be perfect and entire lacking nothing." (James 1:2-4 KJV)

MOSES

By faith, Moses when he became of age refused to be called the son of Pharaoh's daughter choosing rather to suffer affliction with the people of God than to enjoy the passing pleasures of sin. Esteeming the reproach of Christ greater riches than the treasure in Egypt for he looked to the reward. By faith he forsook Egypt not fearing the wrath of the king for he endured as seeing him, who is invisible. (Hebrews 11:24-27)

Moses was a man who grew to his faith potential by fighting many other battles along the way. Moses didn't start out as a faith giant. The Bible says, *"when Moses became of age."* Now that could be naturally, but I like to think its spiritually because he had to come to a place of spiritual maturity to be the leader of the children of Israel. Moses had to grow in his spiritual maturity to reach his full faith potential, not just in his physical age.

Moses battled the pleasures of sin. We read, *"By faith, when he became of age he refused to be called the son of Pharaoh's daughter, choosing rather to suffer affliction with the people of God rather than to enjoy the pleasures of sin for a season."* There's pleasure in sin or we wouldn't do it, and it wouldn't be so hard to resist. Moses fought an inner battle to give up his love for the enjoyment that he got from sin. If we don't slay that giant on the inside, we will be unable to battle much else in life. The Bible tells us that we all struggle with that.

> *Love not the world neither the things that are in the world for the world with the lust thereof shall pass away, the lust of the eyes, the pride of life will pass away but he that does the will of God shall abide forever. (1 John 2:15)*

We are told not to love the world or the things that are in the world because it is the system that Satan designed and is filled with the pleasures of sin. Sin exacts a destructive toll in us - body, soul, and spirit.

> [2]*"Sin will take you farther than you want to go, keep you longer than you want to stay, and cost you more than you want to pay." -* Mark Aulson

DECIDE TO OVERCOME SIN'S PLEASURES

We must make a conscious choice in order to gain the victory over this battle. The Bible says that Moses decided

---

2   *http://www.jesussite.com/resources/quotes/sin/*

in life that he *"...esteemed the reproach of Christ,"* greater than the pleasures of sin for a season (Hebrews 11:26). In other words, he fought and won over sin's pleasures replacing them with love for the things of God. Moses made a choice in his life, he won the war within, and he beat that giant on the inside.

We all have had our sin that we enjoyed. We might have been a pot head, an alcoholic, a pill popper, or a sex fiend, but the short-term pleasures that we got from those things leave us with long-term consequences. We must kill that giant on the inside in order to reach our faith potential. There is a blessing for the overcomer.

> *Blessed is the man that overcomes temptation,*
> *for once he has been approved he'll receive the*
> *crown of life. (James 1:12)*

We can grow our faith to that level where we believe that all our needs are met, our bills are paid, and our bank accounts are full and overflowing even if there's an economic collapse and hyperinflation. We do this by facing the battles that we're dealing with right now, fighting them, and overcoming them one at a time.

MOSES WAS A CHAMPION

Moses, what a champion he was! He led the children of Israel out of Egypt, went through forty years of hardship with those people, brought water out a rock, called for the quail and the people had meat for lunch every day.

He was an amazing man, but he didn't get there without fighting some battles. He battled the inner struggle to break with the world and he battled the idea of reproach when he identified with the people of God. He chose to suffer affliction with the people of God.

By faith Moses, when he had grown up, refused to be called the son of Pharaoh's daughter, because he preferred to endure the hardship of the people of God rather than to enjoy the passing pleasures of sin. He considered the reproach of the Christ [that is, the rebuke he would suffer for his faithful obedience to God] to be greater wealth than all the treasures of Egypt; for he looked ahead to the reward [promised by God]. By faith he left Egypt, being unafraid of the wrath of the king; for he endured [steadfastly], as seeing Him who is unseen. (Hebrews 11:24-27 AMP)

Have you come to that place that you're no longer ashamed to call yourself a Christian publicly? That's a battle we face on the inside. Are we afraid they will find out at work that we are a Christian? Moses said, "I'd rather suffer the reproach of the Christ." There's going to be some reproach, we can't escape it. People are going to want to know why we don't cheat on our spouse, tell vile stores, talk about filthy movies, and condemn people. They want to know why we are not like the rest of them. That's when we need to say, "It's because I am a child of God, Jesus is my savior and I won't do anything to smear His name."

> **ASK YOURSELF...** *Have you chosen to endure affliction? Want to have some big, big faith? Want to be a motivator of other people during hard times? Want to be a person that people look to and say there's just something different about you?*

Moses chose to suffer affliction with the people of God. You must overcome anything in you that wants to keep quiet about your faith in Christ.

> *"....and be ready always to give an answer to everyman that asketh you a reason of the hope that is in you with meekness and fear."* *(1 Peter 3:15 KJV)*

We should live our lives in such a way that people are asking us questions about our life. I remember when I was in Bible College, I worked at a gas station from 6:00 a.m. to 2:00 p.m., for $2.50 an hour. I was the only Christian there. When I was on my break and I had my New Testament out, they zeroed in on me. Right across the street from our gas station was a pornography establishment and at lunch time those guys would run over there, fill up with all those fowl demons, then come back and want to tell me all about it. They couldn't break me down, they couldn't make me cuss, and they sure couldn't get me to go across the street and watch those movies. They picked on me the whole time I worked there, but I never responded. They knew I was a Christian and I'd tell them why I wouldn't give in to the pleasures of sin.

When I got another job and gave my two weeks notice, the boss came to me privately and said, "Would you pray for me before you leave?" He had to have eye surgery. He asked me because he saw the love of Jesus; he saw someone who was willing to suffer affliction for what they believed for Christ. That kind of faith drew him to Christ.

You'll win the people around you if you learn to suffer affliction for Christ. Moses defeated the pleasures of sin and traded love of the world for the love of the things of God. He overcame the fear of suffering affliction with the people of God. That doesn't mean he was stupid. We need to use wisdom and discretion when we witness for Jesus.

If you want to slay giants, split the Red Sea before you and cross over to freedom, and deal with some major opposition standing in your way, you need to be a Moses. God knows we need Christians today who have the faith of Moses, David, Deborah, Esther and the prophets of old.

FIGHT BATTLES ONE AT A TIME

Hebrews 11:26 tells us *"For he [Moses] looked to the reward, he esteemed the reproach of Christ greater riches than the treasures in Egypt."* How many people sell God out for money?

You must slay that giant in your life, too. You must be willing to follow Christ even if you have to live with financial lack for a while, even it means you have to give up some comforts in your life in order to obey God. You might say, "God wants me to prosper," but God wants you to grow in faith first. God wants you to get your heart right first. God wants you to have your priorities right first. He wants you to be blessed and prosper, but He doesn't want to give you abundance because you love it and you can't live without it.

What if God calls you to the mission field, what if God calls you to live on $20,000 a year in Kenya and you're making $80,000 in the States? You have to give up some things to be a missionary in Kenya. What if God calls you to a country where the income is $50 dollars a month? What are you willing to give up? Most people in America are not willing to give up much for Christ.

The Bible says every one of us is going to give an account of ourselves when we stand before the judgement seat of Christ and we're going to be rewarded. There's all kinds of parables about rewarding us for faithful service now in this life. Moses got to the place where he decided, "I'm not living for the now, I'm not living for the moment, I'm living for eternity." That's a giant you must slay on the inside of you if want to have Goliath faith, Moses faith, David faith, and reach your full faith potential.

YOU MUST QUIT LIVING FOR THE MOMENT AND START LIVING FOR ETERNITY.

One day you and I are going to die, and we are going to give an account of ourselves before Almighty God. He's going to ask us, like He did with the man in the parable with the talents, "What did you do with what I gave you? Did you use it just for yourself or did you use it to build and advance the kingdom of God on earth? Did you use your talents for My cause or just your cause?" When you further God's cause, your cause is going to get furthered automatically.

Jesus said, *"Seek ye first the kingdom of God and His righteousness and all off these things shall be added to you"* (Matthew 6:33). In other words, all these blessing shall come upon you and overtake you. You don't have to worry about that.

Are you using your talents and gifts to further God's purpose? That's why He gave them to you. If you use them to further God's kingdom, those are the things you're going to be rewarded for when you get in heaven. Every Christian ought to be involved in the local church and serving somewhere in the corporate effort. Every Christian needs to use their gifts and talents to further the kingdom of God out in one of the mountains of culture in this world to make a difference.

GOD GAVE US GIFTS AND TALENTS TO FURTHER HIS CAUSE NOT JUST OURS.

Moses looked to the reward. There is a big reward. *"Well done thou good and faithful servant, well done."* (Matthew 25:21) God is going to celebrate you in heaven, did you ever think about that? It's going to be a big celebration when He honors you for your faithfulness in this life.

Satan works hard to divert us, distract us, and draw

us away. We are to fix our eyes on Jesus, the author and finisher of our faith. That means His will and ways are our focus in life and prayer, for that matter, is not about what we want but about what He wants. We can become so self-centered that we consume everything for ourselves, but when we can overcome that and live for God and others, we're going to be celebrated in a big way.

"For by faith he [Moses] forsook Egypt not fearing the wrath of the king." (Hebrews 11:26)

How did Moses grow to that faith potential where he could split the Red Sea? It was because he faced Pharaoh ten times and the Bible says his faith grew to where he no longer feared the wrath of the king. Every time he went before the Pharaoh and said, "Let my people go," and Pharaoh said, "No, I will not let your people go," God would send a plague and then Pharaoh would back off. Every time Pharaoh backed off, Moses lost a little bit more of his fear of Pharaoh.

Every time you face your giant and speak God's word to it, you will see the devil back off. When you see him get off of you and release your "FUD" - **F**ears, **U**ncertainties, and **D**oubts. Always remember that your fear of the enemy just weakens, debilitates, and destroy you. Your fear will diminish when you confront the enemy with faith and fight him every step, every battle along the way. You must fight one battle at a time. Each win builds your confidence in what God will do through you when you face and fight your enemy. Remember this: *"For the Lord will be your confidence and keep your foot from being caught"* (Proverbs 3:26).

FIGHTING THE GOOD FIGHT, BUILDS CONFIDENCE; FLIGHT FOSTERS FEAR.

FOCUSING ON CHRIST ADVANCES HIS KINGDOM; DISTRACTIONS DESTROY PROGRESS.

FINISHING WHAT HE GAVE YOU TO DO IS A VICTORY; PROCRASTINATION LEADS TO DEFEAT.

VICTIMS FEAR...VICTORS VANQUISH THE WORKS OF THE ENEMY.

If you have a demon of fear that's not a big issue because we can cast that out in Jesus' name. However, most of us don't have a demon of fear, we have learned and adopted fears we believe protect us from danger. Learned fears must be displaced by faith. The only way we overcome those learned fears is to face them and fight them. Every time we see a battle won, our fear diminishes a little more and our faith grows a little stronger. It took ten times for Moses to get free from the fear of the wrath of the king. Finally, Moses was at the full faith potential where he could stand and face the Red Sea. He faced it, he fought it, and he finished it. He split the Red Sea, they all went across on dry land, while Pharaoh and his whole army drowned in the midst of the sea.

Did Moses finish his enemy? Yes, he did. He never worried about Pharaoh again. He and his army drowned in the Red Sea. Such victory is our potential, too. We have these stories in the Bible and all these illustrations to teach us if we do what Bible people did we can have what Bible people had.

By faith Moses forsook Egypt not fearing the wrath of the king for he endured all the hardships. How did he do it? Moses saw the invisible God. We must speak, think, feel and declare the truth: *"So we fix our eyes not on what is seen, but on what is unseen. For what is seen is temporary, but what is unseen is eternal"* (2 Corinthians 4:18 NIV).

Later in his second letter to the Corinthians, Paul declared that *"we walk by faith not by sight"* (2 Cor. 5:17). How are you to live boldly without fear?

- Walk by faith in the invisible God not in fear of your visible problems.
- Speak what is possible with God not what's impossible in your own strength.
- Trust His word not the lies of the world and Satan.
- Do what's right, at the right time, and the right way so that God gets the glory.

Chapter 3

FINISH IT: PAUL

*No weapon that is formed against you shall
prosper and very tongue which rises against
you in judgement you shall condemn. This is
the heritage of the servants of the Lord, and
their righteousness is from me says the Lord.
(Isaiah 54:17)*

In 1 Timothy 6:12, Paul said to Timothy, *"Fight the
good fight of faith, lay hold on the eternal life to which you
were also called and have confessed a good confession in the
presence of many witnesses."*

As believers, we are fighting a fight of faith, and it's
a good fight because faith is the victory. Faith can win all
the battles of life. If you keep fighting that fight in faith,

you will win it. 1 John 5:4 says, *"This is the victory that overcometh the world even our faith"* (KJV).

WE WANT TO LEARN HOW TO FACE THE BATTLE, FIGHT THE BATTLE, AND FINISH THE BATTLE.

David didn't run from his fight. Moses had to fight Pharaoh ten times. David and Moses had to face and fight their battles to reach their full faith potential. Esther faced death in fighting her fight. Samson finished strong by walking through death to victory. Elijah faced a multitude of false prophets before both his rulers and a nation. Daniel and his friends had to fight a battle with fear in a den of lions and in the midst of a fiery furnace. Paul had to face another kind of battle. He had to fight the inner struggle that we all have to face—wanting to quit and give up.

> *Unless I should be exalted above measures by the abundance of the revelation, a thorn in the flesh was given to me, a messenger of Satan to buffet me, lest I be exalted above measure. Concerning this thing I pleaded with the Lord three times that it might depart from me and he said to me this; my grace is sufficient for you; my strength is made perfect in weakness. Therefore, most gladly I would rather boast in my infirmities, that the power of Christ may rest upon me. (2 Corinthians 12:7-10)*

Paul was saying, "Lord, I'm getting tired of this, can You

just take this away?" If we are totally honest with ourselves, we have all probably prayed that at least once in our lives. What fatigues you in the battle?

- Irrational beliefs
- Lies of the enemy
- Other Christians with ignorant theology or immature faith
- Enemies who want you to fail
- Friends who are more concerned about themselves than you
- Believers who pray for what they want instead of what God wants
- Fear, unbelief, and doubts (called it FUD, if you will)
- Lack of confidence in yourself or God
- Worldly concerns that are self-centered not God-centered
- Distractions that pull your focus from Christ to anyone or anything else

The Lord answered, "No, Paul, I can't because that would mean I would have to take you out of the world or I would have to take the devil off the planet. It's not time to take the devil off the planet and I don't want to take you off the planet because I want you to keep working, so you're going to have to face it."

Paul met the challenge even though he had to face multiple struggles, *"Therefore, I take pleasure in infirmities, [in reproaches, in needs, in persecutions, in distresses], for Christ's stake for when I am weak then am I strong."* (2 Corinthians 12:10). Paul had a whole category of struggles not just one, and maybe you do, too. Maybe you have a family problem, a health problem, and a financial problem all going on at the same time. Even if you have compounded problems, that's no reason to quit.

The Lord told Paul, *"My grace is sufficient for you."* (2 Corinthians 12:9) Paul, there's ability that you don't know of yet that's available to you, so you can overcome any problem you have in every category."

God is saying the same thing to you and me today. God is calling us to face our battles and fight our battles in order to finish strong and get the crown of life at the end of the day. It's not because God wants us to have a hard time, it's because we are in the world with the devil, world cares, and the passions of the flesh, and none of them are going to disappear. We're not going to flee. It's fight or flight, and we stay the course and fight the good fight. So, there is no Plan B. God's Plan A for us is to face and fight each of our battles and keep moving forward on our life's journey toward triumph.

God wanted Paul to reach another level of victory in his life. He wanted him to reach his full faith potential. God wants the same for you. If you quit, you will never reach your full faith potential. It's when you face that problem and fight it by faith that you can reach another level of God's grace and power in your life. You learn to live without fear because you'll eventually discover there's nothing you'll face that you with Christ can't overcome. That's how you develop an overcoming attitude and eliminate those fears. That overcoming attitude is a finishing faith that fights to the finish.

FINISHING FAITH

We know this worked for Paul. Read what Paul says at the end of his life, after he had reached his full faith potential. It's a long passage, but it's worth reading. I call it "Finishing Faith."

> *For I am already being poured out as a drink offering and the time of departure is at hand. I have fought the good fight, I have finished the race, I have kept the faith: Finally, there is laid up for me the crown of righteousness which the Lord, the righteous judge will give to me at that day: and not to me only but also who have loved his appearing. But be diligent to come to quickly for Demas has forsaken me, having loved this present world, and has departed for Thessalonica; Crescens for Galatia, Titus for Dalmatia. Only Luke is with me get Mark and bring him with you: for he is useful to me for the ministry and Tychicus I have sent to Ephesus. Bring the cloak that I left with Carpus at Troas with you come and the books, especially the parchments. (2 Timothy 4:6-13)*

How many of us would be thinking about continuing our studies while we were sitting in a Roman jail, chained to wall, with no coat, in winter, and with rats running around? That's an overcoming attitude! That's a victorious attitude!

> *Alexander the coppersmith did me much harm; may the Lord repay him according to his works: you also must be aware of him for he has greatly resisted our words. But the Lord stood with me and strengthened me so that the message might be preached fully through me and that all the Gentiles might hear: and I was delivered out of the mouth of the lion. And the Lord will deliver me from every evil work and will preserve me for his heavenly kingdom: to be him be glory for every and every. (2 Timothy 4:17-18)*

Paul says, I've been through all of these things, but instead of relief from pain God will see me through the pain for His gain and glory. You and I are victors not victims, conquerors not the conquered, winner not losers, the head and not the tail.

Go through your battles, so you can grow and face what may come in the future and nothing can destroy and take you out. Pop and Country singer, Kelly Clarkson sings, "What doesn't kill us, makes us stronger. Really? Yes, really if God's in it. God doesn't enjoy seeing you go through battles, but because Satan is in this world, you've got to learn to face each one and fight each battle with the weapons He has given you. You need to finish that battle to achieve the victory.

What are the weapons of the Spirit and not of the flesh (Read 2 Corinthians 10)? Try these on for size...

- Praying
- Knowing and declaring God's Word
- Doing what's right (good works) regardless of the cost or the persecution in order to give God glory.
- Praising God for past, present, and future victories
- Practicing patience and persevering
- Agreeing for God's will to be done with other believers

Paul writes, *"And the Lord will deliver me from every evil work and preserve me for his heavenly kingdom."* (2 Timothy 4:18). How did he get to that level of faith where there was nothing he feared anymore? He grew by facing all the previous battles he talked about in Corinth. If he had given in and quit at that point, he would have never gotten to this point in 2 Timothy where he had this level of victory.

David faced his battles, Moses faced his battles, Paul faced his battles and they all fought through them. The reason they were able to face their battles with such confidence was because they knew one great truth. They knew God was with them.

The reason you can face your battles with full confidence is because God is for you, God is in you, and God is with you. These are three dimensions of your relationship with God that you need to understand.

He who did not spare his own Son but delivered him up for us all, how shall he now also with him freely give us all things. (Romans 8:32)

You must have the confident, overcoming faith built on the knowledge that...

GOD IS IN YOU... GOD IS FOR YOU, AND... GOD IS WITH YOU.

GOD IS FOR YOU

"If God justifies you who can condemn you? (Romans 8:38).

God is so **for you** that He sent His Son to die **for you** and take your place and redeem you from the curse of the law. God is for you. That means He justified you and declared you not guilty through the blood of Jesus. God is for you not against you. When the devil condemns you and says you're nothing, you tell him, "God is for me." If the devil tries to tell you you're a looser and you're not going to make it, you tell him, "God is for me, I'm a winner, and I will make it." God is for you talks about what God did for you in Christ on the cross.

He forgave you, He healed you, He delivered you, He blessed you, and He made you righteous. He did all those things **for you**.

It doesn't matter who is against you, because God being for you is all that matters. God wins. Love wins. Righteousness and justice wins. Faith and hope win. God being for you and in you wins!

GOD IS IN YOU

Do you not know that your body is the temple of the Holy Spirit who is in you, whom you have from God and you are not your own, but you are bought with a price therefore glorify God in your body and in your spirit which are God's. (1 Corinthians 6:19-20)

Not only did He do something **for you**, He did something **in you** because, *"If any man be in Christ he is a new creation, old things pass away and all things become new."* (2 Corinthians 5:17) He recreated your spirit and made you a new creation. When He did that, the Holy Spirit came to dwell in your spirit. 1 Corinthians 6:17 says, *"But he who is joined to Lord is one spirit with Him."* John the Apostle writes that He that is in us is greater than he that's in the world (1 John 4:4).

So, God is dwelling **in you** and the Holy Spirit is joined to your spirit. Therefore, He will never leave you nor forsake you, He will be with you until the end of the age.

Get the wrong stuff out of you so that God may fill you with Himself and all of the fruit and gifts you need to overcome. Check off what needs to exit from your life in order for God to fill you...

- ☐ Fear
- ☐ Doubt
- ☐ Uncertainty
- ☐ Painful memories

- ☐ Regret
- ☐ Sin Habits
- ☐ Unhealthy and unholy relationships
- ☐ Abuse, adultery, or addiction
- ☐ Dysfunctional behavior
- ☐ Gluttony and unhealthy nutrition
- ☐ Depression, despair, discouragement
- ☐ Stubbornness and rebellion
- ☐ Attitudes of ingratitude
- ☐ Blame and irresponsibility
- ☐ Excuses
- ☐ Laziness and slothfulness
- ☐ Worry and anxiety
- ☐ _____

(You name the sin(s) that needs to go!)

GOD IS WITH YOU

Then there is this third dimension. Just like you go from babyhood to childhood to manhood, you grow up spiritually in three progressive dimensions. You have to learn the first dimension, God is for you. Then you move to that second dimension, which is kind of your adolescence stage where you know what God did in you and that your body is the temple of the Holy Ghost. However, you must then move to that manhood stage where you realize **God is with you**. With you is different than for you or in you. It means God is with you in a manifestation of His power. His mighty power is in operation in and through you. He's there with you whether you can "feel" Him or not. You know He's in you, but when you realize you have God with you, God's power is manifested in your life. God with you is another dimension of your spiritual growth.

Look at how God anointed Jesus with the Holy Spirit and with power and then He went about doing good and healing all who were oppressed with the devil. The Spirit of God was in operation in the life of Jesus. You can know God is for you and God is in you, but real faith potential is not realized until the power of God is operating in your life. That's what it means when it says, "God is with you." He's in operation and manifesting His power so the works of the devil are wiped out.

WHEN GOD IS AT WORK WITH YOU, SICKNESS IS HEALED.

WHEN GOD IS AT WORK WITH YOU, CANCERS ARE DESTROYED.

WHEN GOD IS WITH YOU, YOU LIVE IN VICTORY.

Thanks be unto God who always causes us triumph in Christ. (2 Corinthians 2:14)

And the patriarchs, becoming envious, sold Joseph into Egypt. But God was with him. (Acts 7:9)

God was in operation in Joseph's life and look what happened to him. Even though he was lied about, he was slandered against by Potiphar's wife, he was locked up in jail, he got all kind of promises of a great future and great destiny, and all hell came against him trying to stop him, the Bible says, God was with him and delivered him out of all his troubles. Deliverance comes when God is with us. The power is in operation and brings about the victorious life.

You never know what God will do once you get in His manifest presence. This is what you need in your life every day. That is the key to victory. It's not enough to know about and talk about it, you've got to experience God with you in your life. That's the victory of the Christian life.

Look what He did with Joseph. He was with him in that prison and delivered him out of all his troubles with the Word of Wisdom and the Word of Knowledge. He was solving riddles and God was revealing things to him supernaturally because the power of God was in operation in his life. They said, "Get that man out of jail and get him up here. That guy hears from God, he's solving my problems." God was operating in his life and it brought him favor even with Pharaoh.

Stop wasting the power that God has given you through the baptism of His Spirit (Acts 1). Refuse to allow busyness to replace being fruitful—bear fruit, more fruit and much fruit through Christ working in and with you.

I AM WITH YOU ALWAYS

And Jesus came and spoke to them, saying, "All authority has been given to Me in heaven and on earth. Go therefore and make disciples of all nations, baptizing them in the name of the Father and of the Son and of the Holy Spirit, teaching them to observe all things that I have commanded you; and lo, I am with you always, even to the end of the age." (Matthew 28:18-20)

Jesus assured His disciples, "I'm going to be with you always, even to the end of the age. [My power will operate with you until the end of the age]." I like to know God is with me, especially when I go into other nations to fulfill the great commission He has designated for me.

A couple of other preachers and I went to Romania one year after Ceausescu was assassinated. They were still trying to form a new government with the Communists still in authority. We went there to preach in a communist prison that held 2,000 inmates. Talk about a hell on earth. We went in there with suitcases full of antibiotics to help these prisoners. We told them, "We'll bring you this medicine if you'll let us speak to some of your men."

They let 200 inmates come in for us to talk to. You never saw anything so pitiful in your life as the paranoid, fearful look on the faces of these men. We preached the Gospel to them and all 200 accepted Jesus as their Savior. We gave all of them a Bible along with the needed medicine. We sent 200 evangelists back into the prison that morning.

Then, for the next several evenings, we preached

meetings to 500 people every night. Every night the place was packed, and people were getting saved. There was such an anointing, it was like a spirit of evangelism flooded the whole area. We would go out in the street, start preaching, and crowds would gather. Churches were formed and that meant a great revival was happening in Romania and we were there preaching right in the middle of it.

I encountered struggles while I was in Romania as well. At 7:00 a.m. one morning, I was lying in bed and suddenly it felt like a knife stabbed me in the middle of my back and my heart went out of rhythm. I got up, because I didn't want to wake my roommate, and went in the bathroom. In Romania, they still use ox carts; there is no 911 and there is no ambulance service. We were in this little Romanian village up in the Transylvanian Alps just over the mountain from Dracula's castle.

I said, "Lord, I know you did not send me here to Romania to die and there's nobody to help me; no 911, and no ambulance, just You."

Immediately, it felt like a bucket of warm honey was poured on the top of my head and flowed down over me. It flowed over my heart and my heart went back into rhythm, I started breathing normally, but the severe pain was still in my back.

God said to me, "When you step off the airplane in New York, the pain will be gone."

I finished preaching the next four nights with the pain in my back, but I was breathing normally and my heart rhythm was good, so everything was cool. I stepped off that plane in LaGuardia and as soon as my foot hit the ground, it's was like someone pulled that knife out of my back and the pain left completely.

You need to know God's power is in operation in your life. God is with you. When God's power is in operation in your life, you can expect:

- Deliverance from your trouble
- The favor of God
- Wisdom for the mission at hand
- Promotion

Christ has set you free from your past so that you can make right choices in your present that will give you a prosperous, hope-filled future. Don't make decisions based on past experience. Yes, learn from the past so you don't repeat former mistakes.

YOUR PAST DOESN'T DETERMINE YOUR FUTURE.

GOD'S PROMISES, NOT YOUR PAST, DESTINE YOU FOR SUCCESS NOT FAILURE.

God was with Joshua, God was with Moses, and God was with the apostles. In fact, God told Joshua, *"No man shall be able to stand before you all the days of your life."* (Joshua 1:5). The devil will send people in your life to give you problems, to be against you, to hinder you, and to try to stop you from completing your mission. You've got to recognize your battle is not with flesh and blood, but against the *"principalities and power, rulers of the darkness of this world, spiritual wickedness in heavenly places."* (Ephesians 6:12)

I've had the devil send people to me that wanted to take me out, slander me, stone me to death, and ruin me in every way you could imagine. Some of them even thought, "Man, I've ruined John Polis." However, when the dust settled, John Polis was still standing. Thirty-six years doing God's work and I'm still standing right here. Why? God is with me and I know it. I understand the operation of God and His Spirit in my life. I have learned how to submit to and work with the Holy Spirit.

God said to Joshua, "You can expect to see the same supernatural in your life that you saw in the life of your mentor, Moses. I'll be with you the way I was with Moses and nobody will be able to stand before you all the days of your life."

Quit fighting with people, quit worrying about what people do and say, bind the devil, and just know that God is with you and His power is going to operate on your behalf. After all is said and done, you're going to be the victor and God is going to get the glory.

GOD IS FOR YOU.

GOD IS IN YOU.

GOD IS WITH YOU.

If you know those three things, you're going to live out your days, long and strong. You're going to fulfil your destiny.

- You will have a fruitful and productive life.
- You will make other people aware of God.
- You will to lead people to Jesus.
- You will to make disciples.
- You will to do everything God created and called you to do.
- You will become more than a conqueror through Christ Jesus.

FIGHT THE GOOD FIGHT LIKE PAUL!

Before you move on to the next chapter, I recommend that you study those things about God's relationship with you.

> **ASK YOURSELF...** *"What does walking with God mean for me?" "What did he do for me on the cross?" "What does it mean to be a new creation of Christ?" "What does it mean for God to be with me?"*

Once you understand those three things, you're going to be a champion for God, just like David. You'll be a mighty man or woman of faith just like Moses, and you will fight the good fight of faith like Paul. Time to move out and fight the good fight of faith!

> *Father, I just want to thank You today for Your great grace and for Your power in operation in my life. Thank You for the three dimensions*

of my relationship with You. Father, I pray for the spirit of wisdom and revelation to come upon my family and that in every one of these dimensions, they'll have a full and complete knowledge and understanding of You. I desire to walk with You like Jesus walked with You, like Moses walked with You, like Paul walked with You, and like David walked with You. I want to walk in the power and demonstration of the Holy Ghost in my life each and every day. In Jesus' name, Amen.

Chapter 4

EMPOWERED BY THE HOLY SPIRIT

God anointed Jesus of Nazareth with the Holy Spirit and with power. (Acts 10:38)

"I'll pray to the Father and he will give you another helper that he may abide with you forever, the Spirit of truth whom the world cannot receive because it neither sees him nor knows him but you know him for he dwells with you and will be in you." Jesus in John 14:16-17

Nobody lives this life alone. None of those whom we have been studying did it alone. Even Jesus won His battles with the help of the Holy Spirit. In John 16:33, Jesus said,

"In this world you are going to have trouble, but be of good cheer I've overcome the world." How did Jesus overcome the world? He was anointed because the Holy Spirit was dwelling in Him. The anointing that came upon Him was the manifested power of God that brought the miracles and the deliverance of problems. He wanted to leave us an example of how we too could operate with this anointing and power in our lives and overcome trouble in this world.

In 1 John 3:8 it says, *"He who sins is of the devil for the devil has sinned from the beginning for this purpose the Son of God was manifested that he might destroy the works of the devil."* Jesus faced His problems, He fought His battles, He finished them, He overcame even the works of the devil, but He did it through the Holy Spirit.

In Luke 24:49, Jesus made a promise He would send this same help to His disciples, *"Behold I send the promise of my Father upon you but tarry in the City of Jerusalem until you be endued with power from on high [until the power comes upon you]."* He fulfilled His promise on the Day of Pentecost. Acts 1:8 says, *"But you shall receive power with the Holy Spirit has come upon you and you shall be witness to me."*

> *"When the day of Pentecost had fully become they were all with one accord in one place. And suddenly there came a sound from heaven as of a rushing might wind and it filled the whole house where they were sitting and the then there appeared to them divided tongues as of fire and one sat upon each of them and*

*they were all filled with the Holy Spirit and
began to speak with other tongues as the Spirit
gave them the utterance." (Acts 2:1-4)*

Jesus kept His promise, the Holy Spirit was sent, and
Peter explains why in Acts 2:32, *"This Jesus God has raised
up which we were all witness, therefore being exalted to the
right hand of God and having received from the Father the
promise of the Holy Spirit he poured out that which you now
see and hear."*

Have you had your own personal Pentecost yet where
something was seen and heard in your life? That promise
wasn't just for the Book of Acts, it wasn't just for history,
it's for today, too. In Joel 2:28 it says, *"In the last days I'll
pour out My Spirit on all flesh."* The promise of Pentecost is
a promise to every one of us.

MY PERSONAL PENTECOST

*God has said, "I'll dwell with them and walk
among them and I'll be their God and they
shall be my people and therefore come out from
among them and be separate says the Lord
do not touch what is unclean and I'll receive
you and I'll be to you a Father and you'll be
my sons and daughters. I will dwell and walk
among them [in them]." (2 Corinthians 6:16-
17)*

I had my personal Pentecost in October of 1981. It all started when I read in the Bible where it says, *"I was in jail and you visited me."* (Matthew 25:36) I thought, "I need to go visit the jail!" So, I went to the Marion County jail and asked if I could come in and show a film. They said I could, so I brought in a Chuck Colson film and showed it to the inmates and several of them got saved.

I asked the jailor, "Can I come back each week and have a Bible study?"

They said I could, so I came back the next week and several men came out of the cells and came down to the basement where they had the dining area. They sat at the table with me. I got in there at 7 o'clock and had to be out of there by ten. At 9 o'clock, I asked those guys if any of them wanted to get saved. Two men prayed and accepted Christ.

Then I asked, "How many of you would like to receive the Holy Spirit?"

Several guys said, "Yeah, I'll take it, whatever it is, I'm in jail, whatever you bring I'll take."

So, I just prayed this simple prayer, "Father, just send the Holy Spirit."

At ten minutes after nine, a literal sound of a rushing mighty wind filled that jail basement. Now this is being watched by video at the guard desk. The police are up there watching what is going on because they couldn't leave me alone with those guys. They're all watching and listening as this wind starts blowing in the basement making a clearly audible sound.

Five men's hands shot in the air, they began to talk in tongues at the top of their lungs, and their hands are waving like tree branches. The wind blew for fifty minutes nonstop until 10 o'clock. Sometimes the wind blew real strong and sometimes it would calm down. When it was strong the louder they got and when it calmed down they're speaking would calm down. The guards were watching this on closed circuit monitors up at the desk. These guys in the basement were soaking wet from the intensity of that experience.

There was a guy standing in the back just watching all of this happening. After this wind stopped blowing and these guys are just sitting there drenched in sweat, he came over and says, "Hey, if I can see a miracle I might believe this."

I thought, What do you think you just saw?

He said, "My friend up on the second deck had bone surgery today. They took bone out of his foot, his foot is all swollen, and he's in a lot of pain. Go up and pray for him and if something happens I might believe."

The jailer came down and I said, "Hey, this man wants me to pray for his buddy upstairs, can we do that?"

He agreed and took me and the other prisoner up to the second deck, opened the cell, and let me walk in. Here's this 6'7" guy, with a crutch up under his arm, and his foot all bandaged up. He's holding his foot up in obvious pain.

I just said, "Jesus is going to heal you today."

He said, "I sure hope so!"

I got my little anointing oil bottle out and as I went to put that oil on his head, I felt the form of a man walk right through me and right into this guy, who was named Clyde. I opened my eyes and looked. I hadn't even prayed, God just walked right through me into him. Clyde never said a word, he just start patting his foot on the floor, looking at it in amazement. It was completely healed! Later, he signed the crutch, gave it to me, and I brought it back to the church. It reads, "Clyde healed 1981."

From that moment, a revival broke out in the Marion County jail. We were in there every week and it spread from town to town until we were in all the prisons around the state. We had a revival for several years and hundreds of men were saved.

The Warden of Marion County jail said, "This place isn't even like a jail anymore."

So many people were getting saved during that period of time, it changed the whole atmosphere inside of that jail.

Later, as I was preparing to preach on "Is Pentecost for Today?" the Lord said, "John, what happened that night in the jail?"

I said, "Well, Lord, the wind blew for fifty minutes."

"How many days was Pentecost after the Passover?"

I said, "Fifty days."

"How many men were filled with the Holy Ghost?"

"Five, Lord."

"Yes, that's the Pentateuch [the first five books of the Bible]. And what was the first miracle the happened after the day of Pentecost?"

"A lame man was healed."

God revealed to me, "John, you had Acts 2 and 3 in the jail basement that night and everything I did in the Book of Acts is going to happen in your life time."

Well, I've seen blind eyes and deaf ears opened. I've seen cripples walk. I have even seen the dead raised right in our church on Morgantown Avenue. There's one thing that's in there that I haven't seen yet and I hope I don't see it. In Acts Chapter 12, they beat Peter up and threw him in jail. I don't know if I'm going to get to skip that chapter or not, but if I don't then the Lord will be with me in jail.

I had a personal Pentecost. You can have your own personal Pentecost where something manifests that you can see and hear, too. The Spirit of God will move upon you in manifestation and demonstration. Then you will preach with a boldness and power like never before in demonstration of the Spirit.

In 1 Corinthians 2:4 Paul said, *"My preaching is not with enticing words of man's wisdom but in power and demonstration of the Spirit."* I was in Scotland preaching and the BBC of England came to me because they heard there was an American preacher preaching up at the Scottish borders. I was heard all over Northern England on the six o'clock news with their presenter. They were trying to trick me by asking me about Oral Roberts. I did not know he had said God was going to kill him if he didn't get $8 million.

They got me on the air and said, "We have an American preacher here bringing religion to the Scottish borders, American style."

Then the first thing they asked me was, "Evangelist Oral Roberts said that if he doesn't get 8 million dollars God's going to kill him and take him to heaven, what do you think about that?"

I said, "Well, if Oral said it, I believe it. He's a man of God and he's never lied that I know of."

Then they asked, "Well, how do **you** do ministry, American style?"

I said, "Well, I don't minister American style, but like the Apostle Paul, my preaching is not with enticing words of man's wisdom, but in the power and demonstration of the Holy Spirit."

Then I gave a testimony, and somebody called in and got healed. After that, the Lord showed me something. He said, "There's going to be two kinds of churches in the last days, churches of sophistication and churches of demonstration." Guess which one I want to be part of?

SOPHISTICATED CHURCHES IMPRESS, ...**GOD'S CHURCH IMPACTS!**

SOPHISTICATED CHURCHES ENTERTAIN MEN, ...**GOD'S CHURCH WORSHIPS, PRAISES, AND GLORIFIES GOD.**

SOPHISTICATED CHURCHES ARE RELEVANT TO THE CULTURE, ...**GOD'S CHURCH CHANGES THE CULTURE.**

SOPHISTICATED CHURCHES INVEST IN BRICK AND MORTAR, ...**GOD'S CHURCH INVESTS IN SAVING SOULS.**

SOPHISTICATED CHURCHES USE PEOPLE AND LOVE MONEY, ...**GOD'S CHURCH**

LOVES PEOPLE AND USES MONEY TO ADVANCE HIS KINGDOM.

YOUR PERSONAL PENTECOST

There are three things we need to do to have God with us. It's the manifested presence of God that releases the power we need to defeat our enemies and destroy the yokes that try to bind us.

> *Therefore do not be unwise but understand what the will of the Lord is and do not be drunk with wine which is dissipation but be filled with the spirit, speaking to one another in psalms and hymns and spiritual songs and singing and making melody in your heart to the Lord. (Ephesians 5:17-19)*

First, we need to let the Holy Spirit have control of our life and that starts with our tongue. On the day of Pentecost, they were all filled with the Holy Spirit and began to speak with tongues and magnify God. This is the first step to letting God have control of your life. In James 3:7-10 it says the tongue is the most unruly, uncontrolled part of your human experience. That's why God says the first thing you're going to do is get control of your tongue. When you are filled with the Spirit, you surrender your tongue to Him and you begin to experience what it means for the power of God to come upon you. You begin to speak with tongues.

You give God your tongue because if you can't give Him your tongue you won't give Him much else.

That's the beginning of God being with you in His manifestation presence. When you have let Him have control of your life and your tongue, you begin to speak in that heavenly language. You bypass your brain, because it's not coming from your brain. The Bible says, *"He that speaks in an unknown tongue, his spirit speaks, his mind is unfruitful"* (1 Corinthians 14:14). Your mind is not producing this. It's being produced by the Holy Spirit and it's your spirit that's praying. Your spirit connects with your tongue. Jesus said, *"Out of the abundance of the heart the mouth speaks"* (Matthew 12:34). If your head controls your tongue, you're in big trouble unless your mind is renewed. But if your new heart from God controls your tongue, you'll get out of your troubles (Read Ezekiel 36:26).

EITHER YOUR HEAD OR YOUR HEART WILL CONTROL YOUR TONGUE.

Your every word, feeling, and action is empowered by God's love that overcomes thoughts of hate, feelings of fear, and action that hurt instead of heal.

LET LOVE RULE

Beloved, let us love one another, for love is of God; and everyone who loves is born of God

and knows God. He who does not love does not
know God, for God is love. *(1 John 4:7-8)*

Once you've given Him control of your life starting with your tongue, the next thing that you and I must do is let love rule our life. The Bible says, *"May the grace of the Lord Jesus Christ, the love of God, and communion of the Holy Spirit be with you all"* (2 Corinthians 13:14). The word communion means to fellowship and to partner with the Holy Spirit. You know if you want to walk with the Holy Spirit, partner with Him in life, and let Him work through you in the supernatural, then you become more compatible with Him. God is love, so how do you become more compatible with God? You walk in love and love your neighbor as you love yourself.

Do not grieve the Holy Spirit of God. (Ephesians
4:30)

If you're walking in love, you're not grieving the Spirit of God. He wants to have fellowship with you, commune with you, and partner with you. He wants to work with you, manifesting God's power in your life. When He works through you supernaturally, this is how no weapon formed against you can prosper. You have the greater weapon.

Be kind one to another, tender hearted,
forgiving one another, even as God for Christ's
sake forgave you. Therefore, be imitators of
God and walk in love, as Christ also loved us
and gave himself for us as an offering and a

sacrifice to God for a sweet-smelling aroma.
(Ephesians 4:32-5:2)

We imitate God when we're kind, tenderhearted, and forgiving. This is how God treats us. We must learn to let love rule in our hearts and minds. I call that fellowshipping with the Holy Spirit. If you're going to get along with the Holy Spirit, then you must be like Him. In order for my wife and I to get along, we have to have significant areas of compatibility or we don't have fellowship. How can two walk together unless they are agreed? So, to have fellowship with the Holy Spirit, we walk in love and we grow in oneness and intimacy with Him. See, people who walk in love are very sensitive to the Holy Spirit because God is love.

> *In Matthew 22:37-40, Jesus said, "You shall love the Lord your God with all your heart, with all your soul, and with all your mind. This is* **the** *first and great commandment. And* **the** *second* **is** *like it: 'You shall love your neighbor as yourself.' On these two commandments hang all the Law and the Prophets." Jude 20-21 reads, "Pray in the Holy Spirit. Keep yourselves in God's love."*

YOU AND THE HOLY SPIRIT ARE GOING TO HAVE SOME INTENSE FELLOWSHIP WHEN YOU WALK IN LOVE.

How do you continually pray in the Spirit and flow in God's love?

LET HIS RIVER FLOW

Jesus said, "He who believes in Me, as the Scripture has said, out of his heart will flow rivers of living water." (John 7:38)

The last thing you must do is let Him flow. When the Holy Spirit comes upon you, let His river flow. He's going to come upon you with the nine gifts of the Spirit. These are the manifestation of the Spirit Himself. He wants to manifest Himself for a purpose.

For the manifestation is given to each one for the profiting for all. To one is given the word of wisdom, the word of knowledge, discerning of spirits, faith, gifts of healings, working of miracles, prophecy, different kinds of tongues, and interpretations of tongues, but all of these of are of that one and selfsame Spirit, distributing to each one individually as he wills. (1 Corinthians 12:7-11)

God is at work in you both to will and to do His good pleasure and purpose. So, when the Spirit comes upon you and manifests Himself, you have to let Him flow. You cooperate with Him and let Him have control, let Him rule your life, and let that river flow. Can you imagine what kind of a life you can have when no weapon formed against you can prosper? Whatever the devil brings, you're going to deal with it as you partner with the Holy Spirit.

I visited Beaufort, SC one week to rest and just wait on God while working on a five-year plan for our church. I was just praying and meditating when I started having some raging symptoms in my body. They were symptoms like I haven't had for a long time around my heart. If I didn't know how to walk with God, I would be dead, many times over. So, I began to pray in the spirit and let God come upon me.

It was so awesome because He spoke to me, and said, "I'm done with that, it's already done. Don't ask me about that, just tell that to get off of you."

So, I told the symptoms to get off of me for two days and then it got off of me and I was fine. I don't have to **get** healed, I'm already healed. I hear the voice of the Lord, flow with it, and do it. It happens not only for healing, but for my finances, my relationships, and my kids. He's with me in my finances. He's with me in my health. He's in our ministry. Everywhere I go, He's with me because I've learned to let Him have control, let love rule in my heart and mind, and then let the river flow.

Let me ask you, what is hindering the Spirit's flow in your life. Will you repent of every hindrance and allow Him to have His way in you and through you? The Spirit's river, flowing through you, not only empowers you like a hydro-electric dam producing electricity; His river cleanses you and washes away every impurity in your life. **Flow, River, Flow!**

Now life really becomes exciting and victorious. As you flow in the river of the empowering Holy Spirit you will discover that no weapon formed against you can ever penetrate your shield of faith!

YOUR PERSONAL PENTECOST

That promise Jesus made wasn't just for the Book of Acts, it wasn't just for history, it's for today, too. In Joel 2:28 it says, *"In the last days I'll pour out My Spirit on all flesh."* That means the promise of Pentecost is a promise to every one of us.

HAVE YOU HAD YOUR OWN PERSONAL PENTECOST YET, WHERE SOMETHING WAS MANIFESTED AND SEEN AND HEARD IN YOUR LIFE?

It's a fact that either your head or your heart is going to control your tongue. It's very important how you answer this question.

WHICH IS IT FOR YOU?

You need to learn to cooperate with the Holy Spirit. Let Him have control, let Him rule your life, and let that river flow. When you do, whatever the devil brings, you're going to deal with it as you partner with the Holy Spirit.

CAN YOU IMAGINE WHAT KIND OF A LIFE YOU CAN HAVE WHEN NO WEAPON FORMED AGAINST YOU CAN PROSPER?

*Father God, thank You that it's **Your** will for me to have my own personal Pentecost. I pray for the Spirit of wisdom and revelation to be upon me as I release control of my tongue and my life to You. My desire is to flow continually in the gifts of the Spirit so that no matter what I face each day, I am fully equipped to handle it through Your Holy Spirit and love flowing through me. Amen*

Chapter 5

NO WEAPON

"No weapon formed against you shall prosper, and every tongue which rises against you in judgment you shall condemn. This is the heritage of the servants of the Lord, and their righteousness is from Me," says the Lord."
(Isaiah 54:17)

Isaiah 54:17 is the great promise given to Israel when they came out of seventy years of Babylonian captivity after they repented of their idolatry. God brought them out according to His prophetic word over their lives. This promise is for us today as well.

There are three things critical to winning our battles

and actually experiencing no weapon formed against us will prosper.

1. The battle is spiritual and therefore we must be strong spiritually to overcome it.
2. We must understand and apply the art of self-defense and exposing the devil's weapons.
3. To finish the fight, we must declare the finished work before it ever happens and then fight through and finish strong.

YOU CAN REALIZE FREEDOM IN THE SPIRIT!

The battle we are fighting is really about freedom. God's message for us is freedom. Jesus said...

> *"The spirit of the Lord is upon me because he has anointed me to preach the gospel to the poor, bind up the broken hearted, preach deliverance to the captives, recovering the sight to the blind, set at liberty them that are bruised, preach the acceptable year of the Lord"* *(Luke 4:18-19).*

God created men and women to be free. However, Satan is fighting to bring you and me back into captivity and make us his servants and his slaves. This is really what spiritual warfare is all about. Either you're going to walk in freedom or you're going to become captive of the enemy.

Going back to David and Goliath, when Goliath came out there to face David what did he say?

> *Then he stood and cried out to the armies of Israel, and said to them, Why have you come out to line up for battle? Am I not a Philistine and you servants of Saul? Choose a man for yourself and let him come down to me.* **If he is able to fight with me and kill me then we will be your servants, but if I prevail against him and kill him, then you shall be our servants and serve us.** *(1 Samuel 17:8-9 emphasis added)*

Goliath represents the devil here and the Philistines represent the enemy's camp. If you and I don't learn how to live in the freedom and the victory that we have through Christ, then we'll be back under Satan's bondage. It's just that simple.

In Luke 10:19, Jesus said, *"Behold I give you power over all the power of the enemy and nothing, nothing shall by any means hurt you."* The phrase "by any means" is judicial and means nothing can legally hurt you because legally speaking you've been redeemed by the blood of Jesus Christ. Satan has no legal right to ever do any harm to your life but he does try. He wants to bring people back into bondage and into captivity.

ARM YOURSELF WITH WEAPONS OF SPIRITUAL WARFARE

Paul explains the nature of our battle and the weapons of our warfare in Ephesians Chapter 6:10-18

Finally, my brethren, be strong in the Lord and in the power of his might. Put on the whole armor of God that you may be able to stand against the wiles [the schemes, the strategies] of the devil. For we do not wrestle against flesh and blood but against principalities, powers, against the rulers of the darkness of this age, against spiritual host of wickedness in heavenly places. Therefore take up the whole amour of God, that you may be able to withstand during the evil day and having done all to stand, stand therefore having girded your waist with truth, having put on the breast-plate of righteousness and having shod your feet with the preparation of the gospel of peace; and above all, taking the shield of faith, with which you will be able to quench all the fiery darts of the wicked one and take the helmet of salvation, and the sword of the Spirit, which is the word of God: praying always with all prayer and supplication in the Spirit, being watchful to this end with all perseverance and supplication for all saints.

The first thing we are instructed to do is be strong in the Lord because the battle is spiritual and belongs to the Lord. In Mark 3:27 Jesus warned, *"Unless the stronger one comes he cannot bind a strong man."* Jesus could bind a strong man because He was stronger. Paul says that we have to be strong in the Lord and in the power of His might because we are wrestling with levels of devils. There are principalities, powers, rulers of the darkness, and a spiritual host of wickedness. These devils have different levels of power and we must have power to meet that challenge in our lives. That's why Paul prayed that we would be strengthened with might in our inner man that we would keep getting stronger and stronger in the Lord. We may be facing a difficult battle to stay free from bondage. We need to be strong spiritually because it's spiritual warfare.

We can become strong mentally, we can grow strong physically, we can become strong emotionally, and we also must be spiritually strong. Spiritual strength grows as we pray and intimately ingest and exercise our faith through knowledge of the Word. Additionally, we need other Christians; we are part of the army of God. We live in communion and fellowship with other Christians. We need one another. In the movie "Gladiator," Maximus said, "If we stay together we will survive." If we are isolated from the group, we are easier to pick off. Roman soldiers knew that and that's why they were so strong. You become strong by your personal relationship with God and your relationships with one another. You must cultivate the vertical and the horizontal relationships to really be as strong as you can be in the Lord.

WHEN YOU UNDERSTAND THAT IT'S A SPIRITUAL BATTLE, YOU REALIZE YOU MUST BE SPIRITUALLY STRONG.

Ephesians Chapter 6 is really a lot about self-defense. People today understand the need for learning self-defense. There are martial arts schools for children and adults because there are more and more challenges out there walking the streets by ourselves. We must learn how to defend ourselves and Ephesians Chapter 6 is about our spiritual self-defense. God has given us weapons to meet the challenges coming against us and exposes the works of the devil.

PUT ON THE BELT OF TRUTH

First, we are to put on the belt of truth. The Roman soldier wore a large belt that went all the way around him. The tools and implements he needed for battle were connected to that belt. The same is true for our spiritual belt of truth. Everything is connected to that, so that's the starting point in preparing for our spiritual warfare.

Jesus said, *"If you continue in my word, then are you my disciples indeed and you shall know the truth and the truth shall make you free."* (John 8:31). We need to know the truth and be full of God's Word in order to walk in freedom. Colossians 3:16 says, *"Let the word of Christ dwell in you richly [not meagerly] teaching and admonishing one another with songs and hymns and spiritual psalms singing and making melody in your heart to the Lord. Whatsoever you do, do it all in the name of Jesus.*"

Sometimes our lives are full of so many things that there's just not enough room to get full of God's Word. Satan has worked his system very successfully to keep people so busy, so away from church, so out of their prayer closet, and so away from their Bibles that they remain weak and are easy to overcome. Sometimes, we have to empty out a little bit in order to make room for what is essential.

Satan is not stupid, he's smart and he knows how to weaken his enemy. He's not only interested in weakening individuals, but groups of people, nations, churches, and families. He wants to take people back into captivity and bondage. His desire is to be God and he wants to have servants.

The thing about serving the devil is you'll never rise higher than servant level, but when you become a child of almighty God, you rise to the highest level. You are in Christ and you have the highest position you could ever have the moment you're born again. You become sons and daughters and joint heirs with Christ from day one.

We then need to grow in the knowledge of God's Word. We have to get full of God's Word. Whatever we do must centered around God's Word. Then when Satan puts pressure on us, he gets blasted with the Word of God! What's in us will come out because, *"Out of the abundance of the heart the mouth does speak"* (Luke 6:45).

I've had this happen in my life over the years. The devil realized I could deal with his low-ranking devils, so he'd send one a little stronger and the battle was a little harder. I realized I had to dig a little deeper, get a little fuller, increase my prayer life, and get greater anointing in my life, so when I speak to that devil I blow him back to hell. I know this doesn't sound like fun, but you've got to understand you have to face the battles of life. You've got to fight the battles and use the weapons God has provided for you. No soldier goes into battle without knowing the weapons and strategies of his enemy and understanding how to use his own weapons.

David had to fight the lion and the bear to prepare him for the biggest battles in life. People are taken out many times because they've failed to face and fight and develop themselves to the place where they can handle that top-level devil or whatever big thing Satan will try and throw at them.

God told Kenneth Copeland as he was praying for more power in his life, "Kenneth, if I gave you more power in your life and somebody pulls out in front of you and you spoke against their car, you'd blow all their tires out."

Satan's weapon of choice is deception. We need to be full of God's truth because Satan is going to try to bring us into captivity through lies and deception. The more we have filled our lives with God's Word, the less chance Satan has of deceiving us and getting us to buy into a lie which will bring us into captivity. In fact, there are three things that Satan will try to use to deceive us.

That we should no longer be children tossed to and fro and carried about with every wind of doctrine, by the trickery of men, in

the cunning craftiness of deceitful plotting.
(Ephesians 4:14)

A Wind of Doctrine. There are all these different belief systems out there. They can't all be right! Jesus said, *"I am the way the truth and the life, no man comes unto the Father except by me."* (John 14:6). It's called the narrow way because He's the only one that died for our sins. Sin is what separates us from God and Jesus is the only one that dealt with that. That's why He is the only way.

The Trickery of Men. Ephesians 4:14-16 of The Amplified Bible says, *"[the prey of] the cunning and cleverness of unscrupulous men, [gamblers engaged] in every shifting form of trickery in inventing errors to mislead."* The Living Bible translation says, *"Then we will no longer be like children, forever changing our minds about what we believe because someone has told us something different or has cleverly lied to us and made the lie sound like the truth."*

The Cunning Craftiness of Deceitful Plotting. 2 Corinthians 11:3-4 says, *"But I fear less somehow as the serpent deceived Eve by his craftiness, so you mind [the battle field] may be corrupted from the simplicity that is in Christ. For if he who comes preaching another Jesus whom we have not preached or if you receive a different spirit which you have not received or a different gospel that you have not accepted, you may well put up with it."* Paul is basically saying Satan will take control of people's mind through deceitfulness and cunning craftiness like the serpent deceived Eve. We need to know the truth because Jesus warned us, *"[The devil] was a murderer from the beginning and does not stand* *in the truth because there is not truth in him, when he speaks a lie he speaks from his own resources. For he is a liar and the father of lies"* (John 8:44). We defeat the lies and deception of the devil by knowing the truth through the power of God's Word in our life.

> *The word of God is living active, powerful and sharper than any two-edged sword piercing even to the dividing asunder of the soul, spirit joints and marrow, thoughts and intents of the heart nothing is hidden before the eye of him with whom we have to do. (Hebrews 4:12)*

When you're full of God's Word, you're a discerner. The more of God's Word you have within you, the more discerning you become and the easier you recognize deceit. You've got to be discerning to recognize deceit. The easier you recognize deceit, the easier you can keep yourself free.

DISCERNMENT CAN...

- See the invisible...
- Unmask the counterfeit...
- Distinguish between absolute truth and half-truths...
- Sort out the wheat from the tares...
- Envision what's possible with God...
- Know who's trustworthy and untrustworthy.

WEAR THE BREASTPLATE OF RIGHTEOUSNESS

The breast plate of righteousness covers your heart. One of the weapons Satan brings against you is sin consciousness. Have you ever had the devil show you a picture of you doing something wrong? You're born again, yet all of a sudden here's this picture of you committing some sin. In comes shame and guilt. Satan wants to keep reminding you of all your faults and failures in order to keep you under condemnation, guilt, and a sense of unworthiness.

> However, the truth is, "If our heart does not condemn us, then we have confidence before God and whatsoever we ask we receive of him" (1 John 3:21).

The breast plate of righteousness just simply means I am the righteousness of God in Christ. Proverbs 28:1 says, *"The wicked flee when no may pursue but the righteous are bold as a lion."* The Amplified version says, *"bold as a lion in spiritual warfare."* The devil likes to show me a picture of me sinning before I got saved. If I see myself that way, as that old sinner, I will never have faith to fight the battles of life. So, when the devil shows me a picture of me committing some sin, I have to show him a picture of Jesus.

Romans 5:17 says, *"For if by the one man's offense death reigned through the one, much more those who receive abundance of grace and of the gift of righteousness will reign in life through the One, Jesus Christ."* God has given me a free gift of right standing. I didn't earn it. Christ is my righteousness. 1 Corinthians 1:30 says, *"Of God am in Christ Jesus, who is made unto me wisdom, and righteousness, and sanctification, and redemption."* He lived a perfect sinless life for me. I don't have to live a perfect sinless life to be accepted by God. It would be impossible for me to live a perfect sinless life, even as a born-again person. God has given me the liberty to make mistakes and fail. We're not given a license to sin, but God knows we're going to sin, so we are told to confess our faults and God will forgive us.

SATAN WILL KEEP YOU CAPTIVE IF HE CAN KEEP YOU IN SIN CONSCIOUSNESS.

BOOT UP WITH PEACE

When it says put on the shoes of peace, it is talking about walking in peace no matter what our circumstances. The Roman roads were really rough. They had to step on a lot of hard, sharp stones, so they had to wear really thick sandals. We walk through some hard things in life, too. The Bible says, *"Great peace have they who love Thy law and nothing shall cause them to stumble [the word stumble means to be offended]"* (Psalm 119:165). Satan's weapon right here is offense. He wants to get you offended at people. He'll bring people into your life to hurt you on purpose in order to get you offended. If he can get you offended, you lose your peace and you become the servant of the devil.

A servant of the Lord must not strive but be gentle unto all men apt to teach in patients with all meekness, instructing those that oppose themselves less peradventure God would grant unto them the acknowledging of the truth unto repentance that they may recover themselves from the snare of the devil, who takes them captive at his will. (2 Timothy 2:24-26)

David was trying to help Saul. He wasn't trying to take Saul's position. He wasn't in competition with Saul, but Saul was insecure and jealous, so he threw javelins at David. People who are insecure are often fearful and jealous of you. You love them, and you believe them to be your friends, but one day they break out a javelin and pierce your heart. They'll do something so hurtful, you just can't believe it. You take offense, you get bitter, and unforgiving. Here's how Satan takes you into captivity.

However, if you learn to live in peace with all men and walk in forgiveness, you remain in freedom not captivity to Satan.

I was helping a pastoring couple, who were both pastors in our network, who had been hurt by their praise team leader. They had done so much to help those people. They groomed them and got emotionally attached. The next thing they knew, the praise team leader said something nasty about the pastor's daughter and then walked out. He was brokenhearted, bitter, and the church lost a lot of people. The night before I was to meet with them, I had two different dreams.

In the first dream, I saw Jesus hanging on a cross just ripped open and bleeding. He's saying, "Father forgive them for they know not what they do." I heard a voice speak to me and say, "You don't have to be healed to love people, you just have to be on a cross."

Jesus wasn't healed, He was hurting, but He could still forgive them in the midst of His pain. We sometimes hear people say, "I just can't forgive them. You don't know how they hurt me." You know that the answer to that is a cross. Paul said, *"It's no longer I that live but Christ that lives in me."* (Galatians 2:20). He also wrote in Philippians 1:21 that for him *"to live is Christ and to die is gain."*

WHEN I DIE TO MYSELF, I AM CRUCIFIED WITH CHRIST, SO MY "SELF" CAN'T BE RULING FROM THE THRONE OF MY LIFE.

In the second dream, I saw people doing mean things to Bill Graham and he's not responding, he just allowed it. The voice said to me, "Billy Graham is gracious. A gracious person lets other people do them wrong."

If you can't walk in peace, Satan will take you captive. If he knows you're easily offended, he's going to keep sending folks in there and keeping you captive. When that temptation comes for you to get offended, say, "I'm going to walk in peace, devil. You're not getting ahold of me."

THE SHIELD OF FAITH

Faith is everything to the believer. Faith is a lifestyle, not something you do when you're in trouble. It's how you live. Take the shield of faith because Satan is going to shoot some fiery darts at you.

The Roman shield was as big as a door, made out of wood, and then covered with some kind of skin. It was soaked when they went into battle because the enemy would shoot burning arrows at them. Since the shield was moist, it would extinguish them. The fiery darts Satan will fire at us could be fear, grief, anger, or lust. Satan will send fear that can be so consuming, we call it a panic attack. It makes one just want to run in terror, take pills, drink alcohol, or take drugs. Thank God we can say with the psalmist, *"I sought the Lord and he heard me and he delivered me from all of my fears"* (Psalm 34:4). Psalm 23:4 says, *"I will fear no evil: for thou art with me; thy rod and thy staff they comfort me"* (KJV). So, when fear comes we have to be able to speak our faith and drive out that fear.

These flaming missiles hit my brain when I was in Bible College. I would sit there and try to get them out of my head. God spoke to me and said, "John, break the silence, open your mouth...you can't think one thing and speak another at the same time. Open your mouth, speak the Word of God and you will drive that thing out. You'll put that fiery dart out. You'll quench the fiery dart of the wicked one." I can tell you, it worked!

WEAR THE HELMET OF SALVATION

*But let us, who are of the day, be sober, put
on the breastplate of faith and love; and for a
helmet, the hope of salvation. (1 Thessalonians
5:8)*

In Deuteronomy 1:21, when they were getting ready
to enter the Promise Land, Moses said, *"Look, the Lord thy
God has set the land before you: go up and possess it, as the
Lord God of your fathers has spoken to you; do not fear or be
discouraged."* Discouragement is another weapon of Satan.
Satan is going to try and get you to take off your helmet
of salvation which protects your mind. Hope is what saves
your soul—your mind, will, and emotions.

*Hope deferred makes the heart sick; but when
the desire comes, [hope comes] it is the tree of
life. (Proverbs 13:12)*

That's why it's the helmet of salvation because it saves
your soul. When you have hope, you don't lose your mind.
When you have hope, you don't come apart emotionally.
It's only when you lose hope that you become a basket case.
The Bible says in Ephesians 1:18 that we can know the hope
of our calling and because we're called to be God's children,
anything becomes possible to us. The more you get in God's
Word, the more hopeful you will become. It doesn't make a
difference what is going on around you.

Hope is based on the promises of God. It is part of
our helmet of salvation against the devil's weapon of
discouragement. According to God's promises, we can do

all things through Christ who strengthens us. Jesus told us nothing is impossible for God. When we have the helmet of salvation on, we don't let the job situation keep us in bondage and fear, no matter what is going on with the economy.

If you're where God put you, there is a provision from God there. Quit chasing provision and find out where God wants you to be, and you'll find the provision that God has for you. As the saying goes, **His vision will come with His provision.** God told Elijah to go sit by the brook. Then He commanded the ravens to feed him there. Then He told Elijah to go the widow's house and He commanded the widow to feed him there. There's a place called "there." Get "there" and say, "Okay God, how are **YOU** going to sustain me here?"

This has been proven everywhere God has sent me. My provision has been there...whether it's been another house in another town or a vehicle to get there...you name it and God provided it.

Once you continually wear the armor of God, you are continually "putting on Christ," and then you will be able to finish strong.

GO WHERE GOD TELLS YOU AND GOD WILL SHOW UP AND SHOW YOU HIS PROVISION RIGHT 'THERE.'

USE GOD'S ARMOR!

Satan's weapons are discouragement, sin consciousness, and deception. All these weapons are revealed by the armor

God gave you to defend yourself, but you must put on the whole armor of God. That is how you live free and not let Satan bring you back into bondage.

Review each of these pieces of armor, define it, and state how they defeat Satan's various weapons.

THE BELT OF TRUTH

Satan's weapon:

THE BREASTPLATE OF RIGHTEOUSNESS

Satan's weapon:

SHOES OF PEACE

Satan's weapon:

THE SHIELD OF FAITH

Satan's weapon:

THE HELMET OF SALVATION

Satan's weapon:

Father God, thank You for the armor and the promises You have provided for me so that I

can walk in victory wherever You send me.
Thank You that I no longer have to live in
bondage to Satan and his lies and deceptions.
Amen

Final Word

FINISHING STRONG

Then David said the Philistine, "You come to me with a sword, a spear and a javelin but I come you to in the name of the Lord of hosts the God of the armies of Israel, Whom you have defied. This day the Lord will deliver you into my hand I will strike you and cut off your head and this day I will give the carcasses of the army of Philistines this day to the birds of the air and the wild beast of the earth, that all the earth may know that there is a God in Israel. And all this assembly shall know that the Lord saves not with sword and spear; for the battle is the Lord's and He will give you into our hands." When the Philistine

rose and drew near to meet David that David
hurried and ran toward the army to meet the
Philistine. Then David put his hand into his
bag and took out a stone and slung it, and
struck the Philistine sinking into his forehead,
and he fell on his face to the ear. So David
prevailed over the Philistine with a sling and a
stone and struck the Philistine and killed him
[he finished it]. (1 Samuel 17:45-50)

David faced his battle because he couldn't escape it. He fought his battle because he knew God was with him. Then he finished it because he had all the weapons he needed to complete his mission! He put an end to it when he killed the giant and cut Goliath's head off (1 Samuel 17:51).

What was David's real sword? Ephesians 6:17 says his sword was in his mouth. What does that mean? He met Goliath's challenge with a declaration of victory right from the very beginning of his encounter with this seemingly undefeatable foe. It appeared David had nothing that could compete with his enemy's intimidating weapons.

"Let me tell you about my weapon," David declared boldly. "I come in the name of the Lord of hosts."

Then David continued his declaration and shows us how to finish the fight. David spoke the end result before he even began the battle.

SPEAK THE FINISHED WORD FROM GOD.

YOU'RE NOT HOPING ABOUT THE
OUTCOME... YOUR CONFIDENCE AND
HOPE IS IN THE LORD.

YOU'RE NOT PRAYING TO RECEIVE AN
ANSWER... YOU HAVE **THE ANSWER!**

BOLDLY ANNOUNCE TO THE DEVIL
AND BEFORE MAN WHAT'S GOING TO
HAPPEN...WHAT GOD **WILL DO!**

> *"This day the Lord will deliver you into my*
> *hand I will strike you and cut off your head*
> *and this day I will give the carcasses of the*
> *army of Philistines this day to the birds of the*
> *air and the wild beast of the earth, that all the*
> *earth may know that there is a God in Israel.*
> *And all this assembly shall know that the*
> *Lord saves not with sword and spear; for the*
> *battle is the Lord's and He will give you into*
> *our hands." (1 Samuel 17:46)*

David declared he was not only going to take out
Goliath, but the whole Philistine army as well. *"So it was,
when the Philistine rose and came and drew near to meet
David, that David hurried and ran toward the army to meet
the Philistine."* (1 Samuel 17:48). David was so sure of the
victory that he ran toward the battle.

Then David put his hand in his bag and took

out a stone; and he slung it and struck the Philistine in his forehead, so that the stone sank into his forehead, and he fell on his face to the earth". So David prevailed over the Philistine with a sling and a stone, and struck the Philistine and killed him. (1 Samuel 17:49-50)

He finished it. **You must finish the race...finish your good fight.** You declare the end from the beginning and you tell the devil what's already been done through the finished work of Christ on the cross. You tell him that you were already healed, you were already delivered, and you were already blessed. When you can declare the finished work of Christ, you put an end to it. You've laid the ax to the root of the tree. When Jesus spoke to that fig tree in Mark 11:12-14, and said, *"No man will eat fruit from you hereafter and forever,"* He spoke the end result.

Understand that I, John Polis, **am not trying** to get healed, John Polis **is already** healed. John Polis **is already** delivered from the authority of darkness. I don't start praying, "Oh God help me." I declare to those demons, you cannot do anything to me because I have already been delivered from the authority of darkness. I'm already free. I declare the finished work of Christ and the victory is achieved.

It's the same with your finances. Don't say, "I'm just praying that God's going to help me meet this bill." Start declaring, *"It is given unto me...'good measures, pressed down shaken together, running over'* (Luke 6:38)...all my bills are paid, my bank accounts are full to overflowing, lack is gone, abundance has come. I'm above and not beneath. I'm the head and not the tail. I'm blessed going out and I'm blessed coming in."

When the disciples came back the next day and saw the fig tree had dried up, Jesus told them, *"Truly, truly I say unto you whoever shall say unto this mountain be thou removed and cast into the sea and shall not doubt in his heart and believe those things he says will come to pass he'll have whatsoever he saith"* (Matthew 21:21-22 KJV).

You see, your **real sword** is what you're saying because your faith is decreeing the end result. Abraham called the things which be not as though they were, he declared the finished work. This is how you finish the battles of your life. You don't have to fight sickness and disease the rest of your life, finish it! Declare the end result and say it's already done. *"Whose ownself bore our sins in his own body on a tree that you, being dead to sin shall live unto righteousness by whose stripes we are healed"* (1 Peter 2:24).

ARE YOU READY TO STAY THE COURSE AND FINISH STRONG?

We have all heard of Billy Graham. He started his ministry in the mid-1940's, and at the age of 27 he began to gather crowds in his preaching services. However, has anyone heard of Chuck Templeton or Bron Clifford? In William Martin's biography of Billy Graham, he says that Chuck Templeton was "the most gifted and talented young preacher of his era." Billy Graham, Chuck Templeton, and Bron Clifford were all young preachers of renown in the mid-1940's. Many authors have recounted their stories, but none better than my friend Steve Farrar in his volume entitled *Finishing Strong.*

In 1946, the National Association of Evangelicals published an article entitled, *The Best Used Men of God.* The article highlighted Chuck Templeton and made no mention of Billy Graham. When Bron Clifford was 25 years of age, he was preaching to thousands of people. Everywhere he went there were overflow crowds. It is reported that by the age of 25, he had touched more lives and set more attendance records than any clergyman in American history. He was tall and handsome, intelligent and eloquent. In fact, he had opportunities from Hollywood producers to play significant parts in many of the Biblical movies that emerged in the late 40's and early 50's.

Yes, we have heard of Billy Graham, but whatever became of Chuck Templeton and Bron Clifford? Chuck Templeton left the ministry to pursue a journalistic career and by 1950 was reported to no longer believe in the Lord Jesus Christ in what one might call the orthodox sense. In 1954, Bron Clifford lost his health and family, and became an alcoholic. At the age of 35, this great preacher died in a rundown hotel room on the outskirts of Amarillo, Texas, of cirrhosis of the liver."[3]

I remembered this story about Dr. Graham as I was writing this final chapter. He went home to heaven on February 21, 2018, as I was writing this book. Billy Graham's

---

3   *http://oshawkins.com/sermons/rebuilders-finish-strong/*

faith prompted him to walk in the armor of God and to stay focused on Christ. He fearlessly faced every weapon formed against him and stood strong against the enemy in the power of the Holy Spirit. Are you walking by faith and not by sight so that you can finish strong?

Faith has nothing to do with the senses, but everything to do with the tenses. Until you're in the past tense, you're not in faith yet. People look at their five senses to determine whether they have it or not. Faith doesn't look at the senses, it looks at the tenses.

The children of Israel went through the wilderness in unbelief and doubt except for Caleb and Joshua. They declared the end results because of their faith in God's promise.

> *"But My servant Caleb, because he has a different spirit in him and has followed Me fully, I will bring into the land where he went and his descendants shall inherit it." (Numbers 14:24)*

Your faith is going to bring blessings to your children and your grandchildren and affect your generations. God doesn't obey us, God honors our faith. When we have spoken the end result in faith, God does what we say.

> *But Joshua son of Nun and Caleb son of Jephunneh, remained alive of the men of went to spy out the land, they lived still. (Numbers 14:39)*

They remained alive because they said they would. They said, "We are well able to go up and possess the land and let us go up now." However, they had to wait forty years for all the unbelieving people to die off and get what they had spoken, "We're going to die, you brought us out to die." God said, "Okay," and they all died.

YOU HAVE TO FACE IT.

YOU'VE GOT TO FIGHT IT.

YOU MUST FINISH IT.

THEN, NO WEAPON FORMED AGAINST YOU WILL PROSPER.

Thank you, Lord for Your word. Father in heaven, I thank You for loving me, for sending Jesus to die for me. I welcome Jesus into my life as my savior and I surrender to Him as my Lord. Jesus, You are my Lord, I yield my life to You. I know You are with me when I face, fight, and finish the tasks I declare that no weapon formed against me will prosper. You have given me to accomplish in Your name. Amen

We walk by the invisible not by the visible. When our faith grows like Moses' faith grew, it will bring us to the place where we are living by the invisible. We live by the inner image, the vision inside of us painted upon the canvas of our heart by the word of God.

That's when faith has reached its full potential. That's when you live by the invisible; by the eyes of your spirit. The Bible, the Word of God has opened the window into the invisible realm for you and that's what you see and that's what you live by.

WHEN YOUR FAITH GETS TO FULL POTENTIAL, NOTHING IS IMPOSSIBLE, BECAUSE ANYONE WHO CAN SEE THE INVISIBLE CAN DO THE IMPOSSIBLE. THAT'S WHERE MOSES REACHED IN HIS FAITH.

WHAT'S KEEPING YOUR FROM REACHING YOUR FAITH POTENTIAL?

Answer the questions below and then begin to implement these powerful truths on building your faith potential so you can become the Moses you are called to be.

- How did Moses grow to his faith potential?
- What did Moses have to battle along the way?
- Why are we are told not to love the world or the things that are in the world?
- Have you come to that place that you're no longer ashamed to call yourself a Christian publicly?
- Or are you afraid they will find out at work that you are a Christian?
- Do you want to be a motivator of other people during hard times?

- Want to be a person people look to and say there's just something different about you?
- Are you using your talents and gifts to further God's purpose?
- Are you living by the invisible?

About The Author

John Polis was saved and filled with Holy Spirit in 1974 during the Jesus Movement. He attended Dayton Bible College and graduated with a B.A. in Biblical Studies in 1980, after which he became pastor of a Pentecostal church in West Virginia.

In 1983, John had an encounter that transitioned him into the ministry of Apostle, afterwards he began to travel as an Evangelist and International Bible Teacher.

Among the works established was Eldoret Bible College, in Kenya, Africa, which was birthed in 1998 and has graduated over 1200 students with undergraduate and graduate degrees. Students have planted more than 600 churches throughout Africa to date, some of which have more than 5000 in attendance. John has been a television and radio host for more than 30 years and has authored 11 books, now translated into 6 languages. As President and Founder of Revival Fellowship International, John, and his wife Rebecca, have many spiritual sons and daughters in 13 States and 5 Countries. John carries and imparts an Elijah Anointing to prepare the Church for discipling nations as mature sons and daughters. John serves on the Council of Elders for the International Coalition of Apostolic Leaders and is a former United States Marine, being a veteran of the Vietnam War. John and Rebecca have been married 43 years with 4 children and 8 grandchildren.

OTHER BOOKS BY JOHN POLIS

How to Produce Abundance In Your Life

Release The River Within You: Increasing The Anointing Flow

Put On Your Gloves: The Five Battles Every Christian Must Win

Apostolic Advice: Proven Wisdom for Building Strong Foundations in the Local Church

Recycled Believers: Solving The Mystery of Migrating Sheep

The Kings Are Coming: Understanding The Kingly Anointing

Biblical Headship: Making Sense of Submission To Authority

The Master Builder: Wisdom for today's Apostles

Take My Yoke Upon You: Fulfilling Your 3 Dimensional Destiny

For these and additional resources to help you in your spiritual growth, go to www.johnpolis.com.

JOHNPOLIS

I N T E R N A T I O N A L

Helping creat and shape great futures
JOHNPOLIS.COM

THE COMPLETE SCHOOL OF THE HOLY SPIRIT

Benefit from 40 years of Spirit filled life and ministry with the new 14 hour course produced by Dr John Polis.

This in-depth study of the Person and Work of Holy Spirit, punctuated with prophetic impartation, life encounters and sound teaching will be an essential equipping tool for individuals and churches.

AVAILABLE ON
USB, DVD, Or CD
$99
+shipping

THE COMPLETE SCHOOL OF THE HOLY SPIRIT

TOPICS INCLUDE: What Faith Is, How Faith Comes, Believing with the Heart, Doubt in the Heart, Fully Persuaded Faith, The Gift of Faith, The Sixth Sense, Destroying Things That Are Not, Faith & Patience, What You Say Will Save You, and more.

Enjoy 13 sessions of a special anointing God poured out upon Dr. John as he ministered prophetically on the subject of faith. Receive revelation and an impartation of the spirit of faith. Over 10 hours of teaching with syllabus included.

AVAILABLE ON
USB, DVD, Or CD $99
+shipping

THE COMPLETE SCHOOL OF HEALING

The Complete School of Healing is the result of more than 35 years of study on the subject of Divine Healing. YOU WILL LEARN ABOUT: A Scriptural Basis for Healing, The Origin and Nature of Sickness, God's Will and Healing, Methods of Receiving Divine Healing, and When God Doesn't Seem to Answer.

AVAILABLE ON
USB, DVD, Or CD $99
+shipping

VICTORIOUS

Isaiah 54:17 says, "No weapon that is formed against thee shall prosper; and every tongue that shall rise against thee in judgment thou shalt condemn." In this 5 part series you will learn the secrets of successful spiritual warfare and defeat the giants in your life.

AVAILABLE ON
USB Or CD $30
+shipping

WANT TO
HEAR MORE
OF DR. JOHN?

Download the free Faith Church
International App by searching your app
store for "Faith Church Int" or by
scanning the QR Code.

REVIVAL FELLOWSHIP
INTERNATIONAL

Revival Fellowship is called to preach
and teach RESTORATION
THEOLOGY to the Body of Christ,
presenting "every man complete in
Christ." This is being done through
meetings, conferences, publications, media and Bible
colleges here and abroad.

A second apostolic responsibility of RFI is in the raising up
of a new generation of spiritual leaders as "spiritual sons
and daughters" who will lead restoration revival as it
continues to the coming of Christ. We offer a credentialing
process that brings people into covenant relationships that
are necessary for impartation to take place.

The Elijah anointing has been imparted to RFI and is the
generational inheritance given to those in covenant
connection with the movement. Those apostolic leaders
with an Elijah anointing are the true spiritual fathers of
today's church. By running with this vision, RFI is fulfilling
the prophecy of restoration in Acts 3:19-21..."Heaven must
retain Him until the restoration of all things." **For more
information go to www.rfiusa.org**

Made in the USA
Columbia, SC
15 May 2021